Presented to:

Alonso Vidal

By:

Date: 12-15-2020

Far too many figures of speech translate incredibly poorly when taken factually.

oß————————ßo

"A little learning is a dangerous thing; Drink deep, or taste not the Pierian spring: There shallow draughts intoxicate the brain, And drinking largely sobers us again." — Alexander Pope

"There is a price to be paid for every increase in consciousness. We cannot be more sensitive to pleasure without being more sensitive to pain." — Alan Watts

"This is an important point about symbols: they do not refer to historical events; they refer through historical events to spiritual or psychological principles and powers that are of yesterday, today, and tomorrow, and that are everywhere." — Joseph Campbell

"Fiction is the lie that helps us understand the truth." — Tim O'Brien

oß————————ßo

How do *you* handle truth?

The Light in the Garden

Finally! Hope for the Outcasts
Rev. John S. Nagy

The Light in the Garden
– Finally! Hope for the Outcasts
Rev. Dr. John S. Nagy D. Min.

Also Author of:

- A Brother Asks –
  Volume 1
- The Craft Unmasked!
- The Craft Perfected!
- The Journeyman Papers
- Building Hiram
- Building Boaz
- Building Athens

- Building Janus
- Building Perpends
- Building Ruffish
- Building Cement
- Building Free Men
- Provoking Success
- Emotional Awareness
  Made Easy

ISBN-13: 978-0-99110947-0

First Printing, October 2020
Published in the United States of America
Book Editing, Design, and Illustration
by John S. Nagy
Etchings by Gustave Doré and
repurposed and augmented by John S. Nagy

Books available through www.coach.net

Dedication

To My Numerous Brothers and Friends:

Jeff, Art, Jim, Nick, Kevin, Cliff, and Dale, who have allowed me to bend their ears over and over again regarding the topics and issues discussed in this book. Our discourses have not gone unnoticed.

To My Two Wonderful Sons:

May you find here and direct the true gift that God has bestowed upon you and all those who you encounter in life's wondrous journeys.

To My Loving Wife:

This is but one of the many culminations brought about from a talk we had years ago and from talks that continue to this day. Your honest understanding and warm-hearted patience support me in those moments that count the most.

SUITABLE and FAIR WARNING

Should you have this book in hand and are preparing to journey forth in partaking of the fruit it has to offer, please understand that the light it has to share may not at first sit well within your current view. This book puts forth, through allegory and metaphor, discourses filled with critical analysis of the events within the Garden in Eden (and without along with the conditions required for re-entry).

For some, this book will be a rollercoaster ride of sensations filled with emotional upheavals and laced with upsets and possible anger. For others, it'll be filled with a continuous affirmation for what was felt all along to be the truth behind its telling.

I'll not apologize for the former and offer only that I hope that if the reaction you have to what is shared here is being upset, before you come to any conclusions, I encourage you to read the entire book through. I believe you'll be glad that you did and that you'll be rewarded for your effort.

For those of you who want to share with others what is revealed within this book, I caution you to do so with only those who have also read it through at least once. To discuss the issues, topics and revelations put forth within it with someone who has yet to read it through is to invite reactions that may be divisive. The book is offered as a whole and the concepts put forth within it are intended to be a part of that whole. Making effort to discuss any section of it without full awareness of how it fits into the whole invites possible misunderstandings that might turn ugly.

Even though this book offers truth for those ready to receive it, I have changed the names to protect the not-guilty and to point you, the reader, toward further light.

May the light offered within it make you free.

Preface

This writing reflects many years of personal & professional deliberation upon the story told in chapters two and three of the book of Genesis.

This book is a fourth complete rewrite of what I first penned over thirty years ago but never published. I was not a published author at that time and I stumbled into writing it quite by accident.

My interest in writing this book was to share the original nuances in the story that have remained unknown to many of those readers who have relied upon whatever translation they chose to settle upon. Consequently, many readers of the Eden story have never had the opportunity to understand the depth of the tale or all the revelations it provides. Therefore, this entire book explores The Word between the words.

I do not claim to be a biblical expert in any way. This was not the intent of this book's writing. In my early years, I chose to seek the truth and wisdom in such writings without investing heavily in their concrete factualness. I found that arguing for or against such things took me away from what I could learn from them. I have faith that you'll be led to whatever Light you need.

Therefore, my focus in this book is upon the meaning and relevance of such texts rather than upon their historical concreteness; treating the text as a strict allegory where revealing truth, and not fact, is the aim. With this Light and intent, I'm led to state quite succinctly that the story told within these Genesis chapters reveals truth, even more so today than ever. It reflects the true will-filled nature of humankind, especially in Western civilizations, contrasted to its collective experience of God.

I have taken great pains to neutrally present this writing, focusing my efforts on not conveying the factualness of the story but only on sharing the truths revealed by it. I know that I have fallen short of my goals in some areas and I thank you ahead of time for your forgiveness of these lacks.

Many of my friends who have read the original manuscript of this book commented on my harsh analysis of two of the main characters, Adam and Eve. A few of my screeners said I should look at Adam and Eve as naive children and be less critical in my evaluation of their behavior. My response to these comments is that it is true that I was relentless in my evaluation. *My choice to be relentless is especially true if you hold to the belief that irresponsible people (such as I consider Adam and Eve to have been) should be allowed to continue along the same path of irresponsibility unchecked no matter what effect their behavior has upon others or themselves.* Most readers shall hopefully gather that I do not hold their behavior in high regard - *figuratively or literally.* Hence, one might easily conclude that I haven't been relentless enough.

Regardless of my care to divest this writing from being taken literally through treating it as allegory, I have no doubt there will be those souls who read this as a personal attack on their beliefs. If you are such a soul, my advance request to you is that you set aside a rush to judgments, patiently wait through any fallacy you may have perceived, and seek to glean *some truth* for yourself that inspires you.

For those of you who see truths in this writing, may you use them to bring back to your part of the world the intended experience of Paradise and life ever-lasting.

Above all, please, enjoy the journey it offers!

The Author

Prelude to Eden

In the beginning... – Genesis 1:1[1]

It was a late-night conversation with a warm-hearted young lady over thirty-two years ago that triggered once again that deep-seated memory of inner spiritual confusion. We had met on a blind date about two weeks earlier and this evening found us talking about many widely separated topics.

There was one topic specifically that reflected a major discomfort for us both. It was that familiar religious message that many others of our faith have heard within their lifetimes. As we spoke into the wee hours of the morning, we continually questioned this message that we had been given by each of our respective religious educations.

What was that message? *It was that children were born with original sin and that they must be in some way washed clean of this sin to make them acceptable in the eyes of God and the community.*

We both had major discomfort with this message. We both believed that newborns could not have sin in any way. In both our eyes we saw any belief that was contrary to this as most unusual. How could newborns, people very sacred, innocent, pure, and special in our eyes, be blemished with sin; especially sin that was not their own? While our ears and eyes had been taught one thing, our hearts were telling us something entirely different from the message that we had been receiving from others. It was our heart to heart talk that evening which helped us realize that we were very much alike in heart, mind, and spirit.

I remember talking with her about what I had concluded many years before regarding the ritual cleansing called Christening or Baptism that I had been told about. I believed at that time, and still do, that the ritual "washings" were more for the parent's sake than that of the children. In my eyes, children are born pure, and that the cleansing ritual was and is more to remind every parent that they are in charge of keeping clean and nurturing young souls that are incredibly special. More specifically, parents were gifted with a pure and clean spirit to nurture and that they were expected to do their best to not mess up or dirty that gift!

Yet, this is not what many within our faith have been told. The dominant message which many of us receive in our varying Christian cultures is that we have all inherited Adam and Eve's original sin and that, as a result, none of us are in the garden within Eden. Many people conclude, from what they have been told about the Bible text, that the original sin brought about a curse or punishment from God. The curse we are told was due to the disobedience of Adam and Eve and that we, as their countless descendants, are "unsaved humans" destined to suffer outside the garden because of this unless a specific intervention took place.

This message was, and still is, reinforced continuously by many of our families, cultures, and societal attitudes. The sad aspect of all this is that although most Christians have read, or at least heard, the first three chapters of Genesis, many have walked away with a less than clear understanding of the intent of what those chapters were communicating. Instead, they have learned bastardized and heavily biased interpretations of the story based upon what others have directly and indirectly told them about what these scriptures say and mean.

While my date and I talked that evening, I had no idea how much I would eventually be challenged many years later by the birth of my first child.

What was my challenge? To seek spiritual confirmation of my thoughts and beliefs that my child, just like all other children, was born pure and without the original sin that so many have accepted as burdeningly real.

The odyssey I chose because of this challenge uncovered a multitude of truths regarding the perception of the original sin which so many Christians claim was our inheritance. What my quest discovered was startling and even more important.

What did I discover?

The perception of original sin currently held by many Christians was a twisted smoke screen that prevents us from seeing the true original sin that first occurred in Eden's garden and which, left hidden and unchallenged for centuries, continues to plague our lives and our world on a daily basis.

Seeking Answers

It was about five years after my talk with my then-girlfriend, now my wife, when I went back to the "Good Book" to investigate and (I hoped) obtain answers to two questions that had harassed me for some time. These questions had come up more than once for us during our conversations in the past. Sadly enough, each of these questions had never really been fully answered to our satisfaction. One might think and hope that they could and would be. The questions were simple and powerful. Fortunately, I was compelled by an inner force to seek answers that were just as simple and powerful.

What were those two questions? They were as follows:

Why were Adam and Eve, two of the main characters in the Genesis story of the garden in Eden, thrown out of the garden?

What was the actual original sin, that everyone was so convinced these two characters committed, that got them tossed out?

I truly believed that I knew the answers to both of these questions. Strangely enough, I've asked many other people these same two questions and for the most part, I've received pretty much the same responses from the majority of them that confirmed what I already thought that I knew.

Those responses to the first question that I received had to do with two central characters of the story, Adam and Eve, being disobedient to another main character, God. As a result of this disobedience, they were punished and banished from the garden in Eden.

There were variations on the answers given to me too. Most of the variations had to do with a deeper interpretation of what the fruit represented; you know, *sex.* Nevertheless,

the main response to the first question always came back the same. Most people believed the reason for Adam and Eve being tossed out of the garden was because they broke God's commandment.

This information did not satisfy me though. No matter how many times I heard the story read or shared, I always came away feeling fuzzy as to that being the actual reason God took this action of tossing them out. I know very well what I was told to believe in parochial school and within all those religion-based classes I took years ago. What I had been told never seemed to sit right with me. I felt that something vitally important was missing and so, my quest continued.

I found myself once again picking up the "Good Book" and perusing through chapter one of Genesis, then chapter two, and then three. It was within Genesis chapters two and three that I found the garden story.

I read the garden story again and again from beginning to end. Each time I did, I began to see a new picture that I had not seen before when I was a child. I also began to see that there was a good reason why others and I had not ever been able to see the picture that was now coming more and more into focus. The fact was that, as I read, I became more aware that I had been afflicted with a blindness that kept me from seeing the truth in the story that I had been reading. As my blindness began to fade, it became clearer to me that the actual truth in the story was hidden right in plain sight! I had been unable to see it before because the blinders of my culturally cultivated perspective of the story had prevented me from seeing it. I had been told and taught repeatedly exactly how I was supposed to see and understand the story. I didn't know any better so I accepted their authoritative word and that is exactly how I learned to perceive it, too!

What was it that led me to realize that I had been looking at the story through societal blinders? It was my coming to realize and accept that I had an immature perception, not only of the story, but of life, especially *my* life, in general. That was the key I needed to unlock my blinders. My immature mindset and all that I had grown up to blindly accept and believe was real and true had locked me into an immature perception of the story. Up until that moment of awareness, I had been locked into seeing the same perspective that Adam and Eve first saw, and hence the fuzziness in my understanding of the story. With the coming of greater maturity though, the picture painted by the garden tale was now made much clearer.

Until then, I hadn't realized the sheer invasive power which my immature perception of these two chapters held in my life and how that view had come to bias how I perceived the world around me. This perspective and the subsequent attitude it had created within me surrounded me and seduced me at every turn. It was there, within the culture in which I had grown up, within the schooling I had received, within the supporting legal system into which I had been thoroughly indoctrinated and yes, even in the well-worn ways of my family of origin.

And it was intoxicating! There wasn't a place in my life where this immature "perspective and attitude" of mine was not alive and kicking, and reinforced. It was toughened by my upbringing, my schooling, and my social circles. It was no small wonder that others, as well as I, had remained blind and chained to it for so long. It was hiding right there, out in the open, and no one had been able to see it for what it was.

This culturally ingrained and supported perspective and attitude was the basis behind the reason for my being unable to see the real original sin for what it was. It was not, however, the perspective which I had come to know through my upbringing. The action in the story which I had been taught was a sin was all intertwined with the perception of disobedience and the breaking of a commandment. The sin that I now started to perceive and understand was wholly different from that of which I had formerly been taught. I had been unable to see it because I had been conditioned to look for something else and to ignore the obvious!

This new way of seeing things tied in intimately with the second question in my search which I posed earlier. What was the answer to the other question – the true reason for Adam and Eve being tossed out from the garden? Amazingly enough, the reason for this was neither what I had been taught nor what I had come to believe.

As I mentioned earlier, that which you hold in your hands is my fourth rewrite of this book. Since my initial efforts to write it, it had become clear to me that my quest was incomplete. I had only posed two questions, and I hadn't yet done what was now obvious: *Pose a third question.*

Never realizing that there was a third question which needed to be asked is what had kept me from finishing this book for so long. I had always felt great discomfort with the idea of publishing it, but I never truly understood why until I matured enough to be able to ask this third question:

If the original sin wasn't what we had first imagined it to be and the reason that Adam and Eve (and by extension, us) were tossed out of the garden <u>was not</u> for disobedience, then what must we do to regain entrance to the Garden and renewed access to the Tree of Life?

And with that question now delivered and understood, what does all this mean for humanity?

⁃⁃⁃⁃⁃⁃⁃⁃⁃⁃⁃⁃⁃⁃⁃⁃⁃⁃⁃⁃⁃⁃⁃⁃⁃⁃⁃⁃⁃⁃⁃

Contents

Part I

The Knowledge Tree

That which we accept blindly
remains hidden in plain sight.

The Good News

"It's showing a plus sign," she said, not quite knowing
what it meant.

I remained silent and reached over to the box to try to
figure it out. "Wait a minute," I finally spoke, as I read
through the instructions.

"What's it say?" she said anxiously anticipating my next
words.

I took a deep breath and scanned the materials for a plus
sign. "Instructions should be *easier* to navigate," I thought
to myself.

"Well?" she asked with a mix of uncertainty and
anticipation.

I turned the instructions over and there it was! A plus-
sign meant a baby was on the way!

I took my eyes off the instructions, directed them toward
my best friend, my wife of nine years, and I smiled. Her
eyes swelled up with tears of joy. After five years of trying,
we were finally pregnant. We hugged and sighed together.

Then she broke our hug off. "Are you sure?" she asked with hesitation, not quite wanting to embrace the joy that should normally follow such good news after all this time.

"Positive!" I said with a facetious grin

She gave me a not-too-gentle love tap and we broke out in spontaneous laughter filled with delight and relief. We had been together for a decade and for over half that time we

had been actively engaged in pursuing parenthood. And on this day, we were finally blessed with knowledge that a new soul was on its way and soon to be a part of our lives.

Our relief was understandable too. We had tried so long without success that we had even consulted fertility experts to explore other options. But after being told everything was in good working order, I decided to go about researching the matter along different lines. In time, my quest provided a worthy path and humorous result as well. When I shared my findings with Candy, we both chuckled and decided to go for it.

What direction had we gone? It was based upon an old joke that had been around for quite some time. It went like this: *What do you call people who practice the rhythm method of birth control?* And the answer is, *"parents!"*

With a giggle and smile, we followed all the rules that people practicing the rhythm method would follow, *only in reverse!* We tracked Candy's temperature daily and when the conditions showed that she was fertile, we did exactly the opposite of what the method espoused – *we engaged fully in hopes that we would be the next couple to be called, "parents."*

And here it was! We had been given a positive result! We were on our way toward that goal and only after the first month of trying this method, with one minor tweak to it of course – *in reverse.* We were elated, feeling extremely blessed and it showed.

Bedlam

At that time I said to you, I am not able to undertake the care of you by myself; – Deuteronomy 1:9

I went to bed that evening with my mind whirling with anticipation. For the first time in my life, I was going to be a dad. The future would bring to me all the experiences of fatherhood that this newborn life would ask of me. I would face all the demands, responsibilities, and consequences which this gift would bring forth and I looked forward to doing this with my best friend. I felt truly blessed.

As I lay back in bed imagining the future, I recalled a conversation with a friend telling me that my primary fatherly responsibility would be to assure the child remained alive till the child turned eighteen. I chuckled as I thought, "If only that were the sole responsibility."

I reviewed our imagined future, combing through all the potential knots I'd have to untangle as they inevitably came up. And kids had lots of knots! I'd have to ensure that good food would be on the table, health care was taken care of, a roof was overhead, and clothes were available as well. So much to plan for...

Education too! Not only the nuts and bolts stuff that a person needed to survive in this world but the tricks and short cuts that our child would need to know so that the learning curve would not be a waste of time.

And disciplines! Disciplines that would assist our child in living a life filled with beneficial consequences and ones that would naturally filter out those that brought unnecessary grief. I'd have to be a role model for every last one of them, as I know kids watch more than they listen. Sure, they might *hear you* but they will most assuredly *watch you* to make sure you practiced what you preached. And then there were morals! Kids are shaped by the morals they see around them.

I tossed and turned to the internal din. I could not quiet the noisy uproar that churned within me. My mind was in overdrive and it would not allow me to sleep. Thoughts of my imagined future poked at me as they kept me from a peaceful slumber.

At one point, I recalled the conversation Candy and I had when we were dating regarding baptism. In the faith of my

youth, it was called "Christening" and it was a sacrament bestowed upon children soon after their birth.

I reexamined our past conversations. Had we already decided what to do about this? Was this something that we needed to discuss once again? The questions nagged at me for some time before I finally rolled over and said to Candy, "Are we going to have our child Christened?"

Candy mumbled something that sounded like, "I thought we already decided this?"

"Good Lord!" I thought. In my drive for an answer, I had disturbed her out of near sleep. I whispered, "I'm sorry Sweetie. I'll let you go back to sleep.

She rolled over and mumbled something that sounded like, "You really should talk with Bob."

"Okay," I said softly. "Sleep tight."

I rolled back over and mulled over what I thought I had heard Candy say. Maybe Bob could shed some light on the answer I seek. He certainly was someone who I could talk with easily about such things. "I'll call him tomorrow," I heard myself saying softly as I placed a mental note on my list for the morning.

Strangely enough, with this simple suggestion from my half-awake wife, I found enough peace in my thoughts to carry me into slumber.

Reverend Bob

Bob was an unusual minister. He had a practical way of looking at things and his heart-felt pragmatism came out through his directness. Candy and I were instantly attracted to his personality when we first met him. We were seeking a holy soul to officiate our wedding and, after many bad experiences seeking such an individual, we stumbled across Bob. We wanted a person who was well-grounded and had a firm connection to what we felt God was all about. He fit our needs perfectly.

I had called Bob the very next day after Candy had sleepily suggested I seek his spiritual guidance. Sure, she didn't say that, but it was clear that Bob could provide it. He certainly seemed made to order for the struggle I was having. When I called, he didn't pick up his phone. So, I left a message hoping he would return my call soon.

As luck would have it, Bob received my message and within an hour he had called back and we set a date and time to talk. He said he'd be ready to discuss the matter as was needed.

When I showed up at his home, it was late afternoon. He was out on his porch, sipping some ice tea while swinging on his prized antique porch swing. He saw me coming up the walk and yelled, "Good afternoon John!" His voice boomed as it carried over the porch railing out toward me.

"Good afternoon, Reverend Bob!"

"Just Bob, please," he responded.

"Okay, Bob."

It was a routine we had gotten into from the beginning. I would address him formally at first, he would insist on me addressing him informally and I would smile and capitulate without any further struggle.

"So, you want to know about original sin, John," he said getting right into the thick of things. He wasn't much for formalities.

"How did you know?"

"You wanted to talk about Christening. Usually, when someone asks about this Sacrament, it's tied to a concern about original sin."

"Well, yes… I guess I do then."

"So, let's open that door."

"Good! I'd really like more light on this," I said in an earnest tone. "I've had this conversation with Candy before…"

"On what?" he interrupted me seeking more information.

"On the Garden of Eden."

"Anything specific?"

"Yes," I said. "What was the actual sin? The story doesn't clarify what it was and most people I know have been told what it was by someone else."

"Ah!" is all that Bob mustered as a response.

"And what was the real reason for Adam and Eve getting thrown out of the garden? Everyone I know says that it was disobedience…"

"And that doesn't make sense to you I'm guessing?" he interjected.

"Exactly!"

"I take it you've talked with Candy about all this?"

"Yes," I replied. "It was in fact one of the first in-depth conversations we had while we were dating."

"Why would you be talking about this on a date?"

"We were talking about the innocence of children and how it seemed odd that anyone would want to wash them based on an assumption that these children were stained by some sin that someone else supposedly committed."

"That's some deep stuff to be talking about on a date, John," he said teasing me for something he knew I tended to do.

"Yes. It was a conversation, though, that revealed to us both how similar our views were about things like this."

"It was a good bonding moment then?"

"Indeed. I think it was one of the first conversations we had where we felt we had similar spirits."

"Then it was a worthwhile one for sure."

"It helped pave the path to our marriage, Bob," I responded. "And now I'm faced with fatherhood and I want to make sure that I do the right thing for my child. I need some light if I am to be the best father I can be."

"If you want that light, John, you have to be totally willing to travel an unsettling path wrought with grief."

"I don't understand. Why must it unsettle me and fill me with loss?"

"Because the light you find along that path will shatter what you thought you knew. It will wash it all away like a sand-castle on a wave swept shore. You're going to lose your confidence when the first wave of light hits."

Bob had an uncanny way of mixing metaphors. I would have preferred he kept along the light theme and indicate my shadows will all fade away or the imaginary building would be... well, come to think of it, I guess the shattering and washing away metaphor actually did work well-enough to get his point across.

I stopped over thinking what he had said and asked, "Will I walk with a better understanding as a result?"

"I guarantee that you'll walk on firmer ground. That's all I can assure you at this point."

"Then I'm all for suffering whatever grief such a path will bring to me."

"Why?"

"I won't be a father bringing up kids in darkness Bob. Having light on this will mean I won't walk in darkness either," I replied. "I've walked in darkness far too many times before and for far too long at times. It's an unpleasant experience at best. I'd rather walk in light than stumble into dark holes of ignorance unknowingly. My family deserves better."

"I agree!"

"So, shatter and wash whatever needs to be shattered and washed."

"Oh, I'm not going to lift a finger in this, John," Bob said. "This is a trip you'll have to take for yourself and through your own efforts."

"Wait!" I protested. "You're not going to be my guide in this?"

'Not in the least. I'm just warning you of what is to come if you pursue your quest for this light."

"Have you any advice then?"

"Yes," he said. "Keep in mind that your search will bring to you many things that conflict with what you've come to understand and believe."

"What do you mean?"

"I mean that the story you're currently living is understood through a child's eyes."

"Ouch!"

"I told you there would be shattering and washing."

"I didn't think it would happen five minutes in."

"You came to me for light, right?"

I sighed in acknowledgment. "Yes. I knew if anyone could get to the point quickly, it would be you."

"Then brace yourself for a delightfully unsettling journey, my friend," he smiled. "The best is yet to come!"

"What's next?"

"I recommend you get used to partnering."

"Partnering?" I asked, not understanding exactly what Bob meant.

"Yes, partnering. You can't easily do this alone. Prepare to partner with others. It'll make your quest a lot more fruitful and bring things to fruition quicker." Bob gave me a wink hoping I would be amused by his "fruity" word-play.

I was more shocked by his comment than amused. I had always felt that quests like this were a personal project that was worked upon as a solo venture. Sure, it could be done with another and that could help speed the process along. But why it would not be able to easily be done alone I could not grasp.

"You look puzzled," he said breaking my concentration.

"I am."

"What are your best thoughts on this?"

"It's a solo journey," I replied.

"Of course it is, John. Why do you say this?"

"Because it's all internal work. No one but me can do it for me."

"All true John," he said adding, "but you're missing the point of having a partner."

"What's that?"

"Support! They don't do any of your work. They only support you in doing it."

"Like a catalyst?"

"Exactly!" he exclaimed. "But there are other perks that they contribute, as well."

"Like?"

"It's very easy to fool yourself. It's more difficult to fool someone else when they may very well have been down the same path you are going down now."

"So, they bring experience to the table. That adds some tremendous value at times."

"And that experience helps shorten the learning curve," he said with another one of his "don't work harder than you have to" winks. "They may also contribute things that you might not have considered along with resources you might not have access to."

"Okay! I get the message," I said recognizing he was going to continue if I didn't agree. "Anything else?"

"Yes. I recommend that you go to church tomorrow."

"Church?" I said, quite surprised at the sudden turn in Bob's directions. "But I want to talk with you more about all this!" I said in a whining moan of protest hoping he would continue the conversation and be that "partner" that he so encouraged me to find.

"Yes," Bob said with a sigh. "And I want to continue this as well. However, please trust me when I say, go to church tomorrow and see me afterward. I'll be a much better partner to you once you've done this, and so will you!"

Not fully understanding the sudden twist, I yielded to his direction. I trusted him unconditionally. He had counseled Candy and me before he committed to performing our wedding ceremony, he had helped us with our vows and he was a stern guardian to our marriage. He was the best soul I knew besides my wife. I said, "Okay, I'll go."

"Good!" he said smiling. "I'll see you tomorrow evening."

"Okay Bob," I replied and headed back home to Candy.

When I arrived home, Candy already had dinner on the table. It was exactly what I needed after talking with Bob.

"Back so soon?" she said with a giggle.

"And yet dinner is on the table already."

"Reverend Bob called me to let you know you should attend the sunrise service tomorrow," she said. "I figured you'd be on your way home."

"You were right," I said as I took in a deep sniff. "Wow! Dinner smells great!"

Candy gave me a warm embrace. We both loved to cook and we often fought over kitchen rights. In the end, whoever got there first got to cook. She won this round.

"How was your talk with Bob?" Candy asked.

"A bit disappointing."

"Why"

"He told me I had to go at this alone."

"And?"

"But then he said I needed partners as well," I said. "It's all a bit confusing."

"That doesn't sound like Bob."

"Yes, I thought the same thing. But I'm sure he's up to something," I responded. Bob had reliable methods of delivering in impactful ways. "He wants me to show up to church tomorrow. I'm sure he has something planned for me."

Candy just smiled. She knew I was on a quest and, from experience, she knew I would not be off of it until I found what I sought.

We finished dinner that evening with discussions about remodeling one of the upstairs bedrooms in preparation for our child's arrival. Candy had a list of honey dos that she ran by me to set up a schedule for the next seven months leading up to the arrival of our joyful bundle.

Our time passed quickly and we were soon into the evening's slumber activities.

Egress

So he drove out the man; and he placed at the
east of the garden of Eden Cherubims, and a
flaming sword which turned every way, to
keep the way of the tree of life. – Genesis 3:24

The next morning found me getting up two hours before dawn. This was not unusual. I liked to have plenty of time to wake up, prepare for the day's activities, and to travel to get to where I planned to go.

I arrived at the church doors with plenty of time to

spare. I was quite surprised by what I found. Bob had never mentioned anything about the church being closed!

I was listless and disappointed. My church was closed and I wanted its sanctuary. Even though the sign clearly said, "Closed for Renovations," I remained near by the doors, staring at them blankly as if they would swing open under the sheer power of my will hoping I would be greeted with a warm smile by the ghosts of my memories.

My head told me that nothing would change no matter how I felt. My heart was not bound by the reality of my situation. The mere presence of the church doors, close but closed, comforted my spirit. There was familiarity with them and they brought back warm memories of many moments of solace, wrought by many years of attending their soulful services.

I sighed in dismay. After what might have been a quarter-hour of contemplation my legs grew weary and I knew there was nothing but memories here holding me hostage to my desires. I turned away with my back to the building that was my usual Sunday home and walked down the steps to the sidewalk where I stopped. I lifted my gaze from off the mosaic walkway and found my eyes looking beyond my immediate situation and off into the distance.

A glitter of sparkling light, glimmering within the wooded area across the street, caught my eye. Its flicker tickled my curiosity enough for me to venture toward it without hesitation.

I had seen these woods from a distance for many years. They were a familiar landmark in my travels to and from the church. They were always off at a distance though – too far off my beaten path to deserve any effort to explore. I'd never given them a second thought before.

Yet, with the doors of my spiritual sanctuary barring my entry, there were before me the trees all spread out creating an alternative path to consider. And the light in the distance beckoned me to explore its shimmering glow that was penetrating the dense foliage.

I checked my time. The sun had barely started to show its face on the morning horizon above the green landscape before me to the East. The sky was still slightly lit with the faces of friendly constellations, clinging to a heavenly canvas, as they looked down upon me. Their collective glow was enough to illuminate my venture down the garden path before me. Even the morning star was showing brightly in the sky, like the sparkle of light reflecting off a highly polished sword whirling in every direction. "That's a plus! Not a bad way to commune with God," I thought to myself as I traveled eastward into the woody embrace of the morning's illuminated offerings.

The path before me didn't appear to be well-worn. It wasn't clearly marked, but there were telltale indications it was tended to on a regular basis. A trimmed branch here and there with demarcations of stones directing one's attention away from brush and other vegetation and toward clearings where travel was easiest. A grounds-keeper had been clearly

33

at play, as even the fallen leaves were sequestered to areas where composting was well-underway.

Further along the trail was an opening between the narrow lines of trees. Two burly, intimidating looking guards stood by what appeared to be an entrance to a deeper part of the garden. As I approached, my fear must have been obvious for the first guard on the left yelled out, "Look! A scared little girlie-man approaches."

"Oh, stop it!" demanded the guard on the right. "You

shouldn't act that way." He then shouted out to me, "Welcome. What brings you this way?"

"I saw the light in the garden and thought I'd investigate," I responded not sure as to why the guard on my left was acting so intimidating.

"What?" said this guard adding "Didn't have anything better planned have we?" He looked over to the other guard and blurted, "He looks like he's lost."

"Be nice now," is all the other guard said.

"We should ask him what he wants," said the first guard.

"In due time," said the other one. He looked over at me and asked, "I take it that you had other plans for this day?"

"Indeed I did," I said, half bewildered by the oddity of the interaction of the two. "I had planned to attend church services this morning but had forgotten to check to see if it was open."

"So, you messed up," said the guard on the left in an almost antagonizing tone.

"Yes, I sure did," I replied adding, "It's my fault too. I usually check these things out in advance and had forgotten to do that this time." I looked over at the friendlier of the two, on my right, and said, "On the upside, I get a chance to have an enjoyable stroll in this beautiful garden… not a bad consequence, eh?"

"Well then," said this guard. "Your timing could not have been better. There's a small gathering down by the garden café that you might find interesting. You can't miss it. All paths lead to it," he said with a smile.

"You're gonna let him in?" the left guard asked in a hinted fury as if I were not even there listening.

"Of course I am," the other guard said quietly. "He met the requirements... now hush!" He then stepped aside and motioned for me to take the path ahead of me.

The first guard looked upset. I was bewildered as to what he was referring, but I felt I shouldn't push the conversation further. I thanked them both and pressed on.

I had only taken a few steps beyond the entrance when I was whelmed by the garden's magnificent view. The trees were majestic and every one of them appeared to be laden with delicious looking fruit. As I surveyed the scene before me, I saw every kind of fruit imaginable.

"It's a delight to see someone so immersed in my work," I heard a man's voice saying cheerfully in the distance. His voice came from behind me but it was loud enough to understand quite well. I turned to see a middle-aged man, dressed in a work vest and overalls, slowly approaching me through the lush foliage.

The Tiller

*... and there he put the man whom he
had formed. – Genesis 2:8*

"Good Morning," I responded. "I was admiring the garden. Is it yours?"

"I wish!" he bellowed joyfully. "I'm the tiller though and I can show you around if you'd like. There's quite a lot to it, and you might miss some of the more interesting bits if you don't know the terrain."

"As luck would have it, I have plenty of time, and exploring with an experienced guide would be awesome," I said offering my open hand to him. "I'm John. What name do you go by?"

"People call me 'Red'," he said as he extended his hand to shake mine.

Red had a firm grasp; one you'd expect from a worker of the soil. His build matched his grip; sturdy and strong from good use.

"What brings you to the garden?"

"Ah! I answered that question just a few minutes ago," I said adding, "That light off to the East grabbed my attention and I thought I'd investigate it."

"Interesting…" Red said under his breath trailing off without any further words.

"Indeed it was," I replied. "I sense that something's producing the light that I might want to know about."

"I'm glad we crossed paths. We don't get many visitors seeking light. Care if I escort you there? I know how to get it."

"Get it?" I thought. Why didn't he say "Get to it?"

"Well?" he interrupted my thoughts with a little impatience. "I don't have all day. Interested?"

"Of course I am!" I exclaimed. "That would be grand! There appear to be many other things to see here as well," I said as I eyed the ripe figs on the tree to my left.

Red saw me eyeing the fruit and said, "Go ahead and eat."

"Really?" I replied, a bit in disbelief.

"Absolutely! All the trees in this garden bear fruit and the owner has given permission for anyone to eat from every last one of them."

"All of them?" I said, curious as to how many there were. "How many are there?" I asked as I reached for one especially plump fig.

"Hundreds!" he said with a proud tone. "And I have tasted from every last one of them at one time or another."

I heard a delightful, "mmmm," coming from my throat as I savored the fig I had just popped into my mouth.

"Quite good, no?" he said with an ear-to-ear grin.

I couldn't say a word. The flavor was exploding in my mouth. I could tell though that he was enjoying my experiencing it as much as I was. That's the pride of a master coming through. He knew how it would taste to me *long before I picked it.*

"No need to talk," he said proudly. "It's pretty obvious you're overwhelmed by its flavor."

I must have been a sight to see. I found myself nodding, giggling, and smiling with affirmation, all at once.

As he stood there watching me take in this one fruit, he glowed with pride. "That's just one of the hundreds you can sample here in the garden," he said breaking the silence.

When I was finally able to say something, all I was able to render was, "This is *amazing!*"

"Indeed!" he responded. "Even after all these years of tilling I still have the same reaction when I partake. This garden has got some pretty potent soil."

"I'll say!"

"You'll find every tree in this garden has the same impact."

"Seriously?"

"Yes. You're spoiled for life once you've eaten here."

"I can certainly understand why. That first taste was incredible!"

"You get used to it," he said with a pride-filled tone.

"It certainly does raise my expectations."

"How could it not?"

"I know I came here for a reason, but this fruit alone could definitely distract me from my goal."

He giggled. "Relax. You'll get there eventually," he said. "Enjoy the journey, my friend."

"That's a good reminder to keep in mind for sure," I responded and changed the focus. "How long have you been tilling here?"

He laughed and said, "It seems like forever. But that's not a complaint. The work is good for my soul and I must admit I was made for this kind of work."

"It's pretty clear that the work suits you, Red," I said. "From the look of you, you're about as buff as can be and I'm sure that the work and the fruit have a lot to do with it."

Red smiled in silence.

"Which way do we go to get to that light?" I said, breaking the quiet.

"It's not too far down the path you're already traveling. Let's get a move on," he motioned as he led the way.

We walked a bit further and I couldn't help but think how beautiful and peaceful the garden was. My quiet admiration for the surroundings didn't go unnoticed. Red started smiling again with an almost impish glow in his eyes letting me know a conversation was about to unfold that I would enjoy.

"Okay!" I said finally. "Why are you so delighted by my enjoying all this?"

"Call it pride if you must. I put a lot of work into all this," he said as he used both hands to motion toward the terrain. "But it's often the looks it gets from strangers that remind me of how special all this is. Your appreciation for it is an absolute delight to take in."

"It's quite an Eden you have here, Red."

"Eden, now that's a subject I can get lost in."

"How's that?"

"Have you ever taken the time to look at the story that took place in Eden?"

"Yes, I have and I always come away with a lot of unanswered questions," I said with an almost frustrated tone.

"Like?" he responded with an expressed interest that pulled me into replying.

Eden

And a river went out of Eden to water the garden; and from thence it was parted, and became into four heads. The name of the first is Pison: that is it which compasseth the whole land of Havilah, where there is gold;And the gold of that land is good: there is bdellium and the onyx stone. And the name of the second river is Gihon: the same is it that compasseth the whole land of Ethiopia. And the name of the third river is Hiddekel: that is it which goeth toward the east of Assyria. And the fourth river is the Euphrates. – Genesis 2:10-14

"Can you explain why those four rivers were mentioned?" I asked. "They seem to be superfluous to the actual story."

"I can't explain it. But I can tell you to what they might refer," Red responded.

"But not why?"

"I think that might become clear to you, once you hear to what they allude."

"Alright," I said in curiosity. "I'll bite!"

"Have you ever looked into the possible meanings of the garden's name?"

"Eden?"

"Yes," he replied repeating back, "Eden."

"I have."

"And what did you find?"

"It refers to a plain and it also refers to a garden," I replied, "which doesn't make sense since that would mean The Garden in Eden was literally a garden within a Garden."

"Unless that was exactly what the story was trying to communicate," he said playfully.

"That would mean that Adam was placed into this garden within a Garden."

"It would. Did you come across any other meanings?"

"I did!" I said with an excited tone. I had spent some time studying this.

"Ah!" he replied. "Good stuff?"

"Yes," I said. "One meaning was *a delightful place.* That came directly from Hebrew translations which referred to *pleasure and delight.*" [2]

"So, the garden in Eden was a literal garden in an already delightful place?"

"That's what I gathered."

"Did you find anything else?"

"Yes," I responded. "There was one odd meaning that I couldn't quite make sense of."

"What's that?"

"It was the one meaning: *a place that is well-watered throughout.*"[3]

"And that didn't answer your question?"

"What question?"

"Why the rivers were mentioned!" Red said with a loud voice as if to say, "Come on, John! Connect the dots!"

"Oh!" I said quite startled that I had not made the connection before.

"Do you not see the connection between that meaning and the mention of the rivers?"

"Well, to be honest, I hadn't thought that part through," I said. "I suppose that 'a garden within a place that is well-watered throughout' would explain the reason for having so many rivers surrounding it. That would make perfect sense."

"Then you not only have your question answered but you've been given *'a why'* as well."

"I guess so…"

"You seem disappointed."

I thought about how I was coming across and replied, "I guess I was looking for deeper meaning in the names."

"Sometimes it's not as deep as the rivers that are mentioned," he quipped as if to poke a little fun at the subject.

The Fruit of the Tree

> *And out of the ground made the LORD God to*
> *grow every tree that is pleasant to the sight,*
> *and good for food; the tree of life also in the*
> *midst of the garden, and the tree of knowledge*
> *of good and evil. – Genesis 2:9*

As we traveled down the path, I figured I'd continue our talk on the garden topic. "What's the deal with the tree of knowledge?" I asked.

"Deal?" he queried back, not having any clue as to what direction I was taking.

"The deal!" I repeated adding, "What exactly was its purpose, Red?"

Realizing the vagueness of my question, he asked back, "Its purpose or its function?"

"Oh! Yeah," I responded understandingly. "I see how my question could be taken in two different directions." I looked at him with a smile and said, "How about we tackle both?"

"Sure! That would be interesting and fun. How about function first?"

"Okay," I said with enthusiasm. "I like your attitude!"

"Thanks. I know that the scriptures are sketchy, at best, when it comes to the actual function." With that, he pulled out what looked like an old tattered Bible, walked over to a huge rock under a tree, sat down, and said, "And I have a nice little resource to pull from if we get stuck at any point! Come, take a seat."

I laughed and thought, "This guy was for real!" I walked over and sat down near to him. "Great!" I said and suggested, "Then how about we first list what we know about it?"

"Okay. We are told only a few things about it. And some of those things are only inferred"

"What *are* we told?"

"That it was a fruit tree in the midst of God's garden in Eden..."

I interrupted him asking, "How do we know it was a fruit tree?"

"We are told that Adam and Eve ate of its fruit."

"Agreed! What else are we told?"

"That it had a companion fruit tree called, 'the tree of life,' in the midst of the garden with it."

"What else?"

"We are told that when God saw that Adam and Eve had eaten the fruit from the tree of knowledge, He said that they had become 'like one of Us, knowing good and evil'," [4] he replied, smiling at the direction the questions were taking.

"Hmmm… curious…" I responded quietly trailing off.

"Curious?" Red chirped in. "In what way?"

"Curious in the fact that they would know good and evil rather than deciding for themselves what good and evil were."

"Ah! Yes," he chimed in. "It doesn't in any way claim or even imply in the story that they would decide for themselves what is good and what is evil. It only says that they would *know* them both. What's more curious is what 'knowing' means in this context."

"What do you mean by knowing?" I asked.

"Knowing can mean a number of different things."

"Like?"

"Well, for one, it could mean that they would be able to experience good and evil."

"How about also *recognizing* good and evil?"

"Yes, that fits as well," he said. "It also might mean that they would *perceive* good and evil."

"Wait!" I interrupted him. "Are you saying that partaking of the tree's fruit caused them *to see* good and evil, as if good and evil were in front of them even when they were not?"

47

"Yes," he said without hesitation. "We must take the tree's biasing influence into consideration."

"Ah! So, 'knowing' implies that Adam and Eve were only *perceiving, recognizing, and experiencing* good and evil?"

"Yes. If they had been deciding what good and evil were, then Adam and Eve would have been determining what good was and what evil was. They were not doing this."

"But knowing good and evil is the precursor to wisdom," I said adding, "and wasn't it Eve who saw that eating its fruit would make her wise?" [5]

"That's what the translations lead us to believe."

"Wait," I quickly said. "Lead us to believe? Are you implying the translations are misleading?"

"They can be. I'll share with you what I have read and you can decide for yourself."

"Okay," I said, almost bracing myself for what was to follow.

"The actual Hebrew word used within the verse at that point translates as 'to be, circumspect, intelligent.' [6] 'to be wise' is not an accurate interpretation though. It's misleading."

"But how is it misleading?"

"It implies that partakers of the fruit would be the ones who *determine* what good and evil are rather than simply *coming to know* what is good or evil. Furthermore, even if we were to accept that the word 'wise' is close enough in meaning to what occurred at that point, nowhere does it convey that the wisdom they might have obtained from eating the fruit would give them the ability to determine what good or evil was. The Hebrew text only implies that they would know what the standards of good and evil were and so they could judge accordingly."

I looked at him while trying to digest what he had just shared. It must have been some heavy stuff to me because I took a long time to comment.

I broke my silence finally. "So, if we take this information we've just discussed to be true, then Adam and Eve were not determining what was good and evil. God had already set that standard. They were merely provided with this knowledge by God through their action of eating the tree's fruit."

"Yes!" Red said enthusiastically.

"Wait a minute," I held my hand up trying to halt any further additions. "This means that they would, through further partaking of the tree's fruit, continue to gain further knowledge so that they could then be able to apply that knowledge toward making judgment calls on everything that occurred in their lives... never dictating what good and evil were but only judging what was good and what was evil based upon the standard that knowledge from the tree provided."

"Yes!"

"So, they weren't dictating what good and evil were. They were only determining what was good or evil based upon God-given standards!"

Red didn't respond verbally at first. He just looked at me as if he were ascertaining whether I fully understood what I had just said. "How did you come to this conclusion?" he finally asked.

"Well," I looked at him with a face filled with thought, "the story says that they knew good and evil. It never said they *determined the criteria.* It only said that Eve saw the potential for the fruit to provide knowledge to *understand* what was good and what was evil." [7]

I then added something I don't think he expected, "This is fun stuff!"

He let out a resounding belly laugh followed by. "I agree! And it's pretty deep as well! I'm glad you made it past those two burly cherubim at the garden's entrance."

I laughed too. "Yes, me as well! What more were we told about this tree in the Good Book?"

"That God cautioned Adam not to eat from it."

"Why was that?" I pried.

"God implied that by doing so Adam's life would change forever."

"But Red, that's not what's written in the story!"

"Yes," he agreed and continued, "But that is what is *implied!*"

"Implied?" I responded almost as if to protest.

"Yes. It's implied by the very structure of the words and supported by the remainder of the story."

"Forgive me for not taking your word for this without question," I said adding, "How did you arrive at this?"

"The first thing that gives this away is the style in which God communicates his warning."

"What style is that?" I asked, curious to make further connections to what we were discussing.

"A style used throughout the Holy Book that uses figures of speech and exaggerations to convey special truths."

50

"Are you saying what God said about dying was an exaggeration?" I asked almost in protest.

"I'm saying that what is written points to exaggeration as a fact."

"How did you arrive at this?"

"Did they die the day they ate the fruit?"

"Well," I said with a half-hearted affirmation. "They surely did not die that day, or any day shortly after that for that matter."

"Did their lives change forever?" he said, pressing for a response.

"Yes. Perhaps it was a spiritual death."

"That's a guess trying to figure out what God meant, isn't it?"

"It surely is," I said without uncertainty adding, "It's got to have some hidden meaning that we are not wise enough to glean in our human condition."

"Or, it's *exactly* what it is."

"A not-so-obvious exaggeration put forth to convey truth?" I asked rhetorically.

"Yes! Exaggeration is a poetic device used throughout the scriptures to convey special truths interwoven within the matrix of the writing and ones that are not so obvious."

"And in that instance, the truth is as you had conveyed?"

"Of course," he said paraphrasing my previous comment, "at the moment you partake of its fruit, you shall perceive yourself to be mortal." [8]

"Whoa there!" I shot back at him. "You've gone from 'your life will change forever' to 'perceiving yourself to be mortal!'"

"Yep," he giggled, "I surely did."

"Why?"

"Eating the fruit of the tree of knowledge changes your perception."

"Okay, I follow you. But, you took a leap, in your restatement."

"Yes," he agreed. "However, God's exaggeration includes both."

"What do you mean?"

"Eating the fruit changes your life and you shall perceive your life to be mortal."

"You keep using that word 'perceive'," I commented on Red's choice of words. "Why do you use this specific word?"

"Because it's obvious from how the story unfolds that the moment they ate of the fruit, their eyes were opened and they started perceiving all sorts of things."

"Like?"

"Like being *naked* for one," he said with a strong emphasis on the word, "naked."

"Okay. I can see where you're going with this."

"Good!"

"They were obviously naked before the fact. It was only after they ate the fruit that they were able to perceive they were without clothing."

"Yes," he agreed, adding, "or eating the fruit makes your clothes disappear!"

I laughed and said, "I have had a few things I've ingested that have done just that for me!"

"But I don't think that this is the case," he continued, "There was no mention of clothing until after they ate the fruit and it's safe to assume that they, being just created, didn't have any clothes at this point."

"I'll not contest this assumption or conclusion since it does seem obvious based upon how the story unfolds."

"Are you agreeing with me on the impact the tree's fruit had upon their perception?" he asked, trying to establish a foundation upon which we both could move the conversation along.

"Yes," I agreed. "It does appear from what the story conveys that the moment the two partook of the fruit, they started seeing things differently."

"Almost like their lives were changed forever?"

I laughed. "Okay, I now see how you got there. They didn't die. But they did see things differently and this shift is conveyed throughout the remainder of the story."

I felt that we were at closure in our conversation but sensed that there was something still missing though. Reviewing our most recent exchange I hit upon it and asked, "What about that last thing you threw in about them perceiving themselves to be mortal?"

He smiled and said, "I was hoping you'd come back to that."

"Well?"

He held his hand up motioning me to hold on as he pulled a bottle of tea from his pack, and opened and sipped on it slowly, savoring it in the moment. Refreshed he said, "They did not know what actual mortality was before they ate the fruit. How would they comprehend what it meant to 'surely die?' Would the warning that God gave mean anything to a person ignorant of what death was?"

I was silent. His question took time to settle in and he did not press me to respond. I finally broke the lull saying, "I suppose they would not have had the capacity to understand it at any level since they lacked the knowledge to understand God's words prior to eating the fruit."

"Agreed, but it is clear from the interactions between God and Adam before the fruit incident that Adam had some understandings."

"Do you mean when he commented to God about Eve's creation?"

"Yes," he responded adding, "Adam had enough knowledge to recognize Eve had come from him and he used that knowledge to name her. How could he have had that knowledge before eating the fruit?"

"Maybe it was revealed to him through simple observation?" I responded, indicating there might be a *disconnect* between the premise and the outcome.

"Wasn't he asleep when all this was occurring?" he asked pausing while he searched for the words to express his thoughts. "Unless God had created him with an innate ability to comprehend what was unfolding before him, Adam would not have had the capacity to comprehend Eve's creation."

"So, we have to assume from how the story in the Good Book is presented that Adam was created with *some* capacity to understand things as they unfolded."

He shrugged as if to communicate my assumption was as good as any other that could be offered up. "But you have yet to address the two things we agreed we would discuss."

"Ah!" I said with glee. "The function and purpose!"

"Yes!"

"From what we have reviewed, what would you conclude to be the function of the tree?"

He sat there contemplating what I had asked, reviewing our conversation, and even flipped through chapters two and three of Genesis as he thought through it. It took a few moments before he said anything and I was glad that he did. I also needed a few moments to think about it, since I knew he was going to ask me my thoughts as well.

☙————————❧

The Purpose

... God created the heaven and the earth.
– Genesis 1:1

Red broke the silence with, "I'd say the function was to gift mankind with contrast."

I looked at him blinking like a deer in headlights. What on God's green earth did he mean? After a few moments of consideration, I conceded to him, "I have no idea what you're saying."

"John, what was God doing in the very beginning?"

"Creating!" I said hoping I was somewhere near the answer he was looking for.

"Yes. But what was He creating?"

"Heaven and earth?"

"And?"

Knowing that I was onto something, I continued the trend in my answers, "Light and dark, land and sea, sea and sky, man and woman, and sex."

"Exactly! Contrast, John; God was creating *contrasts*!"

"I see what you're saying. But what does..." and I stopped in mid-question.

"Oh! I see that you're onto something," he said with a smile. "Continue your thought."

"I was going to ask what that had to do with the purpose of the tree, but the answer is obvious."

"And?"

"It was a tree that creates the ability to experience, understand, and perceive contrasts for anyone who partook of its fruit. This included the contrast between good and evil."

"Was that its purpose, John?" he asked, making me say what was already understood.

"Well, if it wasn't the purpose, I'd be hard-pressed to come up with another reason," I said somewhat frustrated that I had not seen it before.

"Are you saying God put the tree in the garden so that Adam and Eve could perceive contrasts once they ate its fruit?"

"I think that *you* are, saying it" I replied giving him a wink of assurance that I knew he was asking a rhetorical question. "It's clear to me that what you're saying is that there is a direct connection between God's creating contrasts and His putting the tree of knowledge in the midst of the garden. Furthermore, you're implying that its purpose was to create either the perception of or the awareness of contrasts within those who ate its fruit."

"But you're describing its function, John," he stated adding, "not its purpose."

"What's the difference?"

"Function is how it operates. The purpose is the reason for its function."

"Oh! That's an entirely different point to consider. Purpose..." I said trailing off. I immediately found myself thinking of reasons that could explain the tree. "Could it be something to do with what God wanted for mankind?"

"Like a gift of ability?"

"Yes! God had been doing all the contrasting from the beginning. Why not gift mankind with that ability as well?"

"It would make for an excellent companion to free-will would it not?"

"Excellent?" I blurted. "It's more than that! It would make for a *necessary* companion for free-will!"

"What do you mean?" Red asked.

"How can you possibly be fully able to express free-will without the knowledge provided by the tree to support it?"

"I don't think that you can."

"Then the tree was a gift whose purpose was to help mankind maximize their collective ability to exercise their free-will."

"Then why the warning against eating from it?" he asked adding, "Especially if it was a gift?"

I stared at him as if I was staring out into space. I was once again lost in thought. I had finally become clear on the tree's function and purpose and now this – *a road block!* What could possibly be an explanation for the prohibition of a God-given gift?

And then it hit me! I recalled something I heard in my youth; during puberty to be more on point.

Sleeping Together

And God blessed them, and God said unto them,
Be fruitful, and multiply... – Genesis 1:28

"But I had thought the tree of knowledge was about sex," I said with some hope that Red would shed some light on this.

"It is, but, as we had discussed, it's about far more than just sex," he said.

"So, you're agreeing that it was about sex?"

"I'm agreeing that sex was one of many things it was about."

"I'm talking about the claims that the forbidden fruit was about sex, and that partaking of its fruit is just a euphemism for *having sex.*"

"Yes. I've heard that claim many times before."

"So that's 'yes' you agree?"

"Let me be succinct. I have heard the claim and I do not agree with it. It's not valid or supported."

"Why is it not?" I said in protest. "Why can't it be a metaphor for sex?" I asked demandingly.

"Oh, it can be if you force that interpretation into the mix. I have heard a lot of justifications for the claim. But none of them are supported by the context of the chapters and what was claimed previously, or afterward."

"What do you mean?"

"Well for one, why provide all the apparatus for making babies if you were not going to use them to make children?"

"You mean reproductive organs?"

"Exactly!" he exclaimed. "Other than the pleasure they occasionally offer, they're pretty useless for anything other than what it takes to produce babies. They're not thought of as anything particularly pretty so we can rule out them as being aesthetically pleasing," he said with a facetious grin and giggle.

"I hadn't thought of it in that way," I replied trying to keep a serious tone.

"And then there are those two dead giveaways written in the chapters in question and the one that is presented previously to these chapters."

"What are you talking about?"

"In Genesis 1 it says that God told them to go forth and multiply."

"So?"

"Think about it," he said with a directing tone. "How were they supposed to go about multiplying without having sex? Is there some other method involved that wasn't written down? Was there a process that we were supposed to find out about through other channels? Did God change His mind or did He somehow forget to tell us?"

"I don't know…"

"Indeed!" he interrupted me and added, "All the evidence says that we were equipped from the very beginning to reproduce and to do that operation a man and woman must join together to become one."

"Wait! Is that what it meant at the end of Genesis 2 when it said, *'For this reason a man will leave his father and mother and be united to his wife, and they will become one flesh'*?"

"You're offering it up. What do *you* think?"

"Overall, I think the claim that partaking of the tree's fruit means having sex simply doesn't bear fruit," I said with an evident giggle.

"Is it even barely plausible?" he asked with a smirk.

"Not even," I laughed and then came back to what he said originally. "How can it not be about sex when you said originally it was about sex and many other things?"

"Because you meant "sexual intercourse" when you used the word 'sex' originally and I meant the differences between the two sexes when I responded to your query."

"Ah! The same word being used to convey two entirely different meanings."

"Yes! This is an example of truncated communications. When you are not specific in what you're trying to say, you are going to have all sorts of misunderstandings based upon other people's personal biases and interpretations."

"Isn't that one of the things that makes these chapters so difficult to comprehend?"

"Yes, and when you communicate using *metaphors*, and more specifically *idioms,* [9] you add the possibility of further misunderstandings."

"Are you implying that the Bible uses metaphors and idioms within it?"

"I am," Red replied adding, "and furthermore, scholars say so even more directly than I do." [10]

"Really? Is there an idiom used within *this* story?"

"Yes! The tree of knowledge uses one."

"Do you mean the tree of knowledge of good and evil?"

"Precisely! That's *an idiom* being used right there!"

"Is that *not* a proper translation?" I asked curious to see what he would offer up as evidence.

"It's a *direct translation*. But, because it's a literal translation of an idiom, *it's not a proper interpretation.*"

"I don't understand what you're saying. Would you please explain further?"

"Sure. It's just like the term 'sleeping together' that is used today as an idiom for 'engaging in some sort of sexual relations.' It is an idiom and it has nothing to do with sleeping. Get it?"

"Yes, thanks! I am following the idiom reference better. How does this apply to the tree?"

"The term 'good and evil' was translated directly from a Hebrew idiom giving us what was written word for word in Hebrew. But in the culture of that time, this term, 'good and evil,' actually meant 'of all things' [11] to those within that culture who heard it. Please keep in mind that this was an oral tradition within an oral culture and this story was written down long after it had been first communicated."

"So, are you telling me then that Adam and Eve ate the fruit of the tree of knowledge of all things?"

"No. The *story* says this *all by itself* when it's properly written to communicate what was originally intended."

"So that's why you said the tree is about much more than just sex?"

"Yes. The tree is about the knowledge of all things and that claim would obviously include all things sexual."

Part II

The Original Sin

A tempting shell game

Let the Feast Begin

But of the tree of the knowledge of good and evil,
thou shalt not eat of it: for in the day that thou eatest
thereof thou shalt surely die. – Genesis 2:17

"I think we've gotten off track here," I said, trying to bring the conversation back to that ban.

"Okay. What did you want to get back to?" Red asked.

"The prohibition! Didn't God command them not to eat from the tree of knowledge?" I asked with unwavering conviction.

"God told only Adam that he could eat from *every* tree in the garden." [12]

"Yes. But he was also told not to eat from the tree of knowledge," I fired back.

"Actually, the command was that Adam was free to eat of all the trees and that was pretty absolute. That was an inclusive and absolute statement."

"But God prohibited Adam from eating from the tree of knowledge!"

"That's an assumption on the part of the reader."

"It's a fair assumption based upon what occurred to Adam and Eve after they ate from the tree," I retorted, a bit miffed that I was unable to make a point valid enough to put the issue to rest.

"Only if you assume that eating from it was prohibited and that the consequences for eating from it were bad," he

65

said, apparently wanting me to make some connections that were not so obvious to me.

"But eating from the tree was prohibited and the consequences were bad!" I exclaimed with a little bit too much assurance.

"Those are the assumptions that'll get you into trouble," he said smiling and looking like he hoped that I would take my thinking to the next level.

"Are you claiming that eating from the tree of knowledge was not forbidden?"

"No. I'm saying that the scriptures did not forbid it."

"But it clearly says that God forbade it!" I exclaimed.

"Did it?"

"Good Lord, Red," I said with disbelief, "what part of 'thou shall not eat' don't you understand?"

"Oh, I understand that totally. I also understand that it is *a warning*. It was *not a restriction*."

"What!?" I exclaimed in shock. I couldn't believe what he was saying.

"Think it through, John."

"I have!"

"Then you understand that the first part of what God said was absolute and the second part was merely a warning."

"I'm unclear on this. Would you explain it to me?" I asked, trying to get traction on the connections he shared.

"Sure! Let me walk you through it. The first part is an absolute, as in, Adam was free to eat of all the trees. This is backed by what was written in Genesis 1:29."

"One twenty-nine?" I replied, not making the connection.

"Yes," Red said as he started quoting it. "And God said, 'See, I have given you every herb that yields seed which is on the face of all the earth, and every tree whose fruit yields seed; to you, it shall be for food.'"

"Every tree?"

"Yes. Every tree! This would mean that the Genesis 2:17 statement had to be a warning of the consequences of eating from a specific tree."

"You're claiming it was not a prohibition?" I queried not trying to quibble as to whether the fruit of the tree of knowledge actually contained seeds, or not, thinking that a lack of seeds would invalidate his claimed support.

"Not me," he said quite firmly. "It's the construction of the scripture that's saying this."

"A warning?" I asked still trying to grasp what he was sharing.

"Yes. It had to be a warning of consequence [13] since the first statement was an absolute." [14]

"You're telling me that over all these years scholars have lied to us about the prohibition?" I said almost trying to get him to admit that scholars had either lied to us or were just plain wrong.

"What I'm saying is that common sense and logic tell us that what was communicated to Adam was a statement of permission [15] coupled with a warning [16] that, should Adam choose to exercise that permission fully, he would have a consequence. I don't have to rely upon others to back me up for me to believe that my observations are right."

"So, you admit that your conclusion is not backed by the opinions of scholars."

"I admit only that my conclusion is based upon what is written in the Bible and not on the opinions of others."

"You weren't kidding around when you said that you could get lost in this story," I said with absolute glee.

"You appear to be a kindred spirit in this," he replied with a smile. "Come!" Red said motioning with his hands. "We have some traveling to do and I have someone I want you to meet."

"Who's that?"

"His name is 'Sligh,'" he said. "He helps me out at times and I think you'd enjoy meeting him."

We both got up from our stony seats and he led me further down the garden path, with me picking and savoring the available fruit along the way.

Liar!

And the serpent said unto the woman,
Ye shall not surely die: – Genesis 3:4

Within a short time, Red and I came upon someone who looked like another tiller. Red leaned my direction and said, "John, this is the guy I was telling you about."

"Sligh?" I asked to confirm.

Sligh shouted out, "Yes! That's me!"

I was quite surprised that this guy responded. I thought that he must have excellent hearing to take notice of his name being spoken at such a distance.

"Sligh," Red said as we approached him. "This is John and he's seeking the light he saw from outside the garden."

"Ah!" Sligh responded. "And he made it past the two burly cherubim without losing any limbs. Wonderful!"

He and Red laughed, and I joined in as well, not really thinking it was too funny a joke.

"He's quite interested in that light, my friend, and I can tell you that he'll talk you into sitting a spell if you want to bring up Eden."

"Oh my!" Sligh said with a seriously playful tone. "Interested in Garden chat, are we?" He looked at me like he was about to engage in some tomfoolery.

"Now take it easy on him, Sligh," Red said. "He has an appointment with light in the garden today, and I wouldn't want to have his ears bent too much before he gets there."

"Not a problem!" Sligh said, looking me up and down as if to assess something that I was not privy to.

"Good," Red said as he started to walk away. "I need to tend to some business elsewhere for a few minutes; do you think you can bring him a little closer to the light for me?"

"It would be an honor!" Sligh said with vigor grabbing my shoulder firmly. "Slide this way my friend!" he said to me as he motioned with his body the direction we needed to go.

I followed his direction and we were soon heading down yet another path.

"So, you like Garden chat? What did you and Red talk about that would have had Red tell me this?"

"We were talking about the purpose and function of the tree of knowledge and we were just getting into God's prohibition…"

"Ah! The warning!" Sligh said as if he had discussed this many times before.

"Hold on," I interjected. "I said that it was God's prohibition. Why do I keep on hearing that it was a warning?"

"Perhaps those who have talked with you today have concluded differently," he said flippantly as if the issue was not up for debate. "So, did you discuss the serpent's truth yet?" he asked, almost deliberately changing the subject.

"Wait?! What?!?" I asked bewildered as to what he just stated.

"The fact that the serpent didn't lie," Sligh said as if it were a matter of fact. He then looked at me and asked, "You sure you want to spend our traveling time on this?"

"But the serpent did lie!" I exclaimed ignoring his question. Admittedly, I sounded more indignant than I wanted to come across.

"Ah! I see that you *do* want to talk about it! Good for you! And exactly what was the lie?" he responded sounding like he was sure he knew the answer." He picked up his pace a bit as we continued on the path.

"The serpent said that they wouldn't die!" I insisted as I started to feel a little winded from the trek.

"Well, did they?" he responded rhetorically so I would disclose the obvious without taking liberty.

"Did who?" I said not wanting to respond with a no.

"Did Adam and Eve *die*?" he asked assertively.

"Yes!" I retorted.

"Ah! Specifics! Let me add: In the day they ate the fruit?"

"They became able to."

"Able to die?"

"Yes!"

"So," he took a deep breath and prepared to respond to my claim, "they only *became able* to die, so that made the serpent a liar?"

"Yes!" I said as if he were finally getting what it was that I was trying to communicate.

"And it took *how many years* for them to finish their dying?" he said with a bit of sarcasm in his voice.

"You're missing the point, Sligh! They became mortal the moment they disobeyed God and ate the fruit."

71

"So, they didn't *die*. They just became *mortal*."

"Yes!" I said as if I had won some valuable prize. "You get it!"

"What I get is that the serpent didn't lie."

"He said that they wouldn't die!" I took a breath and continued, "That's a lie."

"But they didn't die, and that's the whole point."

"They did die!" I echoed, as if by saying it repeatedly made it a known fact.

"What's your point?" he asked giving me every opportunity to prove him wrong.

"The serpent said that they would not die and they eventually did."

"He said that they *shall not surely die,* and therein is the problem."

"What problem?" I asked in a confused tone.

"His statement was true in that it was stated within context and it presumed that the reader would understand that context without assumptions and projections."

"Wait a minute," I replied with a bit of hesitation as if contemplating whether I wanted to continue down this line of reasoning with him or not. "Assumptions? Projections? Context? What the heck are you saying?"

"The words used within the serpent's statement echo God's warning – *thou shalt surely die.*" [17]

"And?"

"Those words were directed to Adam within a specific context 'in the day' or, in other words, 'at that moment.' We know from what is written that their deaths did not occur immediately or physically."

"But by their disobeying God and eating of the fruit, they became mortal at that moment!" I stated with an undue emphasis as if trying to convince myself more than him.

"You're assuming that they were immortal *before* they ate the fruit, when all indications within these chapters say that God didn't create them that way," he said hoping I would know my scriptures well enough to get past my self-imposed dead end.

"God created perfectly," I said with firm resolve.

"So, you are assuming that Adam and Eve were perfect when they were created?" he asked half-goading me on.

"Of course they were perfect!" I responded thinking that he had finally gotten my point.

"But they were not perfect as you have classified them…" he started to continue but was interrupted by my

asking the question he had been hoping I would ask.

"Not perfect? What do you mean?"

He smiled, and replied, "First off, if they were perfect, they would have been mature adults, already knowing all that they needed to know," he said adding, "but they were not yet *complete*, or perfect, in that knowledge. They required additional input from the tree of knowledge."

"But they didn't need that input Sligh," I blurted. "All they had to do is listen to and obey whatever God told them.

"How would they have known to listen and obey if they didn't know better in the first place?"

"What do you mean?" I asked not knowing where he was going with his question.

"The tree provided knowledge they didn't have. Without eating the fruit of the tree, how would they know that they should obey because it was *a good thing* for them to listen and obey?"

"God told them!" I said trying to once again drive the point home. "That instruction from God should have been enough."

"Yes. But if God did tell them, how would they *know* that it was *good to listen to and heed God's words* if they had yet to receive that knowledge for themselves so they would know *what* was good or evil, to begin with?"

I looked at him blankly, blinking several times trying to drive his question into my mind and I remained silent in my contemplation. To his credit, he gave me the time I needed to digest his question. He recognized the look. It was one he had probably seen many times before in the faces of those who had to get past their own preconceived notions that, upon consideration disconnected them from reality. I was

74

there now, in the catacombs of my mind searching for a response that would sound plausible and shore up my previously unwavering beliefs. My internal struggle to find an answer was obvious and he gave me as much time as I needed to consider the ramifications of his question.

"It's a paradox, Sligh," I said after much thought.

"In what way is it paradoxical?"

"You're saying that for Adam and Eve to know that it was good to listen to and obey God, they would have to eat the fruit since it would provide the knowledge for them to know better," I explained. "On the other hand, if they didn't eat the fruit, they would not *know* that it was important to obey."

"That's exactly what I've been trying to say," Sligh said with relief. "They were not perfect in that they were incomplete. They lacked the necessary foundational knowledge vital to understand for themselves the important information God had provided Adam, much less obey anything."

"I'll have to think on this, Sligh. But you did say, 'first off', right?"

"Yes, I did."

"Does that mean there's more?"

"Yes. If Adam and Eve were already immortal before they ate from the tree of knowledge, what was the need for the tree of life?"

I went into that glassy catacomb stare again. It didn't take me as long to come out of it this time and he was surprised at my response.

"I don't know."

Not wanting to miss an opportunity to go deeper he asked, "Do you recall the purpose of the tree of life?"

"Of course I do. From what the scriptures say, eating its fruit would cause one to live forever."

"Forever…" he said trailing off.

"Your point, Sligh?" I asked impatiently.

"Forever means: everlastingly, continuously, and never endingly. If they were already perfect, or as many would claim, immortal, what would be the point of having the tree of life in the garden?"

"You're asking me to state its purpose?" I said, almost trying not to answer the question.

"Yes," he said with stern and deliberate affirmation that he wanted my answer.

I mentally scrambled for words. My eyes darted back and forth as if I were trying to imagine something within my head that I was seeking visually and I knew from Sligh's eyes that my failure to find it was manifesting itself unconsciously in my body language. It didn't look like I was finding what I was seeking and I soon turned the question around on him in desperation. "What's *your* answer?" I asked as if I had gotten the upper hand.

"They *were* perfect human beings. Even so, they were created perfect and still lacked both knowledge and immortality. They had the potential to obtain them both by partaking of each tree that God offered them, should they choose to partake," he replied looking back at me with quiet resolution.

"That's not what a lot of people come away with, Sligh," I said almost dismissing the validity of his words.

"Yes," he said affirming my statement. "Very few people think deeply enough about what is written in the story to ever get to the point where they dare to question those who have taught them otherwise. But let's get back to lying."

"Oh, yeah," I said half-shocked by being brought back to our original topic.

"Did the serpent lie about Adam and Eve not dying?" he reasserted his question.

"He half-stated the truth, and that's deceptive."

"Only if you want to believe he was intending evil when he chose to keep his comment brief."

"What do you mean?'

"We often don't say the entire train of thought behind our words when we talk. The serpent's comment was stated at face value based upon God's warning that they would surely die the moment they ate the fruit." He took a breath and let what he said sink in for me. He continued, "The fact is, not only did they not surely die at that moment or in that day when they ate the fruit, but we read that they both continued to live on for quite a few years beyond that moment or day."

"I see what you're saying," I admitted.

"Thanks," he interrupted. He didn't give me an opportunity to continue and said, "Let's go a bit further. Did the serpent lie about God knowing what would occur to them if they chose to eat the fruit [18] of the tree of knowledge?"

"Well," I said nervously, "he didn't lie with that information."

Driving an uncomfortable point home, he said, "So, then the serpent spoke the truth about what God knew, yes?"

"Oh, now you're just having fun with me Sligh," I replied knowing that he had made a point.

"It appears that the serpent didn't lie at all. It appears that most of those who claim that he did lie are looking to blame him for how Eve responded to his words. What's more, people who typically don't connect the dots usually want to view his statements as deliberately misleading Eve."

"It is the serpent's fault," I said without allowing Sligh's comment to truly register with me.

He smiled, almost suspecting that I was going to bring up the serpent's first words to Eve. "Go ahead. Tell me what he did that had so many people conclude that he lied."

"He asked Eve if God really said that they shall not eat of every tree in the garden," [19] I said smugly hoping he would understand now that I was right about the serpent's untrustworthiness.

"And?" he responded apparently fully aware that I expected him to make some assumptions about the serpent's question that would justify my mistrust of it.

"It was a manipulative question, Sligh!" I blurted. "He was testing Eve to see if she really knew what God had said."

"Apparently, she thought that she knew. Well, mostly."

"Mostly?"

"Yes, mostly."

"You say that as if there was something she didn't know."

"She said that they would die if they just touched the fruit."

"Your point, Sligh?" I insisted.

"Who was the first one to tell a lie in the story?" he fired back.

"So, you're implying that Eve lied first?"

"No, but you're demonstrating exactly the problems that come with having an incomplete understanding of what people say," he said with a smile.

"What *are* you talking about, Sligh?" I replied confused as to what direction he traveled off toward.

"I asked you who lied first and you focused narrowly upon Eve and the serpent. You didn't include Adam or God in seeking an answer."

"Why should I? At this point in the story, only Eve and the serpent are present. So?" I replied defensively.

"Just as you assumed in your response that I was talking about only Eve and the serpent, most people take literally the words God spoke regarding the consequences of eating the fruit. They do not understand that they were meant metaphorically. As a result, you have whole books written about what God meant by His words so that their literal interpretation could not be a confirmation of any lie."

"Wait?" I said with a bit of reserved contempt. "Are you saying it was God who lied first?" I asked with abated breath waiting for him to say something I could find fault with.

"If you assume that God's words meant that Adam and Eve would die instantly when they ate the fruit," he replied, "then it is obvious what was said was a lie. Especially since they didn't die the moment they ate the fruit…"

"But…" I tried to interject but he continued.

"Because it is obvious that they didn't surely die, we have to make sense of this disconnect in order to explain how it could be true because God doesn't lie."

"Make sense as in becoming mortal?" I asked.

"Exactly! And we know 'becoming mortal' can't be true since all evidence points to the fact that they were not immortal and needed to eat from the other tree in order to continue in that direction if they wanted to live forever."

"So, we're left with the question of what God meant still unanswered," I said with resignation.

"Not really. When we examine the words within context, looking at what actually did occur to Adam and Eve at the moment right after they ate the fruit, it becomes quite clear what God meant to communicate in his warning."

"And what's that?"

"At the moment Adam and Eve ate the fruit, their thoughts and lives changed forever. Their naivety and ignorance died, not them. And in that moment, their lives ended in one way and they were reborn to another."

"Good Lord! I've heard that before! You've given me a lot to think about here," I said feeling almost like I wanted to put the conversation to rest and move on.

"Thank you," he replied knowing full well that the seed had been planted. It was now up to me to nurture it into fruition or leave it be.

Under the Influence

*For God doth know that in the day ye eat thereof,
then your eyes shall be opened, and ye shall be as
gods, knowing good and evil. – Genesis 3:5*

We continued to move silently down the garden path toward the light I sought. It was clear to me that Sligh appeared to be pretty knowledgeable about what I was looking for. I wondered what more he might offer. I found myself asking him, "What's up with that tree's fruit?"

"That's an interesting question. Why do you ask?"

"It appears to be a focal point of the Garden story. It must have been some powerful fruit."

Sligh stopped in his tracks and didn't say anything. He then motioned to me to come with him off the trail. I followed and we soon found ourselves in the midst of a clearing with a huge fruit tree in its center. Sligh spoke, "This tree has been here for so long that no one alive remembers it being planted."

I looked at it and was in awe of its apparent age and size. I looked in between the branches to get a closer look at its fruits. I didn't recognize what type of tree it was since the fruit looked strange to me.

Sligh saw my bewilderment and responded to my statement. "The tree of knowledge's fruit is extremely powerful, John."

"But why?" I responded, wanting to know what influence it could possibly have just from eating of it.

"It's because the very nature of the fruit changes the consciousness of those who eat it," Sligh said reaching up and snatching a fruit from the tree. He held it up to the light filtering through the tree and said, "By eating from it, one's awareness of things is altered irreversibly." He then lowered the fruit down and toward me and offered it to me saying in a taunting voice, "Go ahead and take it if you dare!"

I knew what he was implying by his gesture and his words. He was re-enacting with me the scene of the serpent's temptation of Eve. I felt uncomfortable and found myself resisting his not-so-subtle urging. "I don't believe what you're saying about it. How can eating some fruit be that impactful?" I asked. I wanted more information before I committed myself to partake.

"Okay! It's really simple. Let's go over it." He was showing great restraint in his tone as he prepared himself to go through an explanation I was sure he had shared before. "If you took a drug that was designed to depress you, what do you think would happen once you took it?"

I played along, hoping the point he was working toward would make sense to me eventually. "Well, I would think I would get quite depressed, no?" I replied almost as matter of fact.

"That's right! And if you took a drug that was designed to create within you a tremendous bliss, what would you think would happen once you partook of it?"

"That's easy my friend." I said with a confident grin, "I would experience a great sense of happiness, contentment, and joy."

"Good!" he said with eager excitement, "You're getting the trend. Now let's say there was a very special designer drug that, once taken, created within the person now under its influence a whole different and complete manner of seeing things. By its very specific design, it would create a new *awareness* within the partaker.

"Would this occur instantly?"

"Of course not. Things like this take some time. That awareness wouldn't be very apparent at first, particularly to the person under the influence. The first symptom would appear as a subtle shift in perception. Since it would have to start simply, it would create a polarized view of the world for the person under its influence."

"Polarized? Like all things perceived by the influenced person would be either black or white, good or bad, right or wrong with no shades of gray in between, no color, only two dimensions?" I asked as I looked for confirmation.

"Yes!"

"Is this not what occurs to people who are on the threshold of emerging awareness?"

"Exactly! They become aware of extremes." He then threw a question my way, "What would be the first thing to happen to such a person just entering the earliest stages of this drug's influence?"

"Wow!" I said, thinking I was finally getting what he was saying, "They would come across as very judgmental in their manner from that point on. They would be really difficult for others to relate to since most of what they were now seeing would be distorted by the drug's influence and not truly what was before them. The influence of the drug would prevent them from seeing the true big picture."

"Indeed!"

I chuckled adding, "Of course, they would have no trouble getting along with some of the others who were also under its influence if the judgments they expressed were in sync with the judgments of those others."

I found myself wanting to ask Sligh something else that might have been obvious to him. "Then wouldn't it be wise to avoid taking this drug at all costs?"

"That's a great question" he commented in a pondering pace. "I've got one for you, too. How would you know if it was wise or not if you were totally unable to be aware of what being wise was prior to taking the drug?"

"You'd likely not know."

"Likely? Why not?"

"Because you'd lack the very foundation of awareness needed to make that determination," I responded.

"So, without the tree's impact…"

"Which was?"

"Cultivating awareness."

"So, you'd not know what was necessary to make an informed choice!" I exclaimed, more for my benefit than his.

"Yes! But if you didn't want that impact to happen to you, how would you know not to partake of the tree?"

"I wouldn't. No! I *couldn't* know."

"But you're not dealing with the obvious issue," Sligh said, looking at me with his hand still holding the fruit out to me.

"What's that?"

"Knowledge is inventory, not power."

"What do you mean?"

"The tree of knowledge was jam packed with inventory that was life-changing for anyone who partook of it."

"I don't understand," I said trying to make sense of Sligh's directions.

"Think about the following. What's going to give you greater ability or empower you more, knowing that you could eat the fruit in front of you or knowing where to go to get the fruit that's in front of you to eat?"

"Obviously it is the latter."

"Why?"

"Because once what is in front of you has been eaten, you now have to go find your next meal."

"Yes! And which is more powerful, knowing where to go to get your next meal or in the case of a tree which bears highly desirable fruit, preparing the soil so that your next meal comes to you?"

"That's obvious, also; the latter of the two choices."

"What do you think about all this?"

"I think what I'm hearing in between the lines, is that the fruit of the tree of knowledge is not a physical fruit."

"Please, expand your thoughts on this if you would."

"Knowledge is not physical," I replied. "It's not just any tree that offers this kind of non-physical fruit. It's any time knowledge is offered to you and you take it that you partake of its fruit."

"And what happens to anyone who takes that knowledge in?"

"That information now transforms the person's view of any situation where that knowledge applies."

"Meaning?"

"By eating its fruit, a person's view of things is forever changed, especially in relation to the knowledge offered."

"So, do you have the answer you sought about the power of that knowledge tree?"

I didn't respond to Sligh at first. I let the conversation settle into my mind. I could see from this conversation that I was no longer looking at the tree of knowledge as one that existed within the garden. I now saw that it was any knowledge offered to me from any source.

Sligh didn't press me for an answer. It was clear to him that I was now seeing things differently.

He tossed the fruit over to me and winked. I caught it, looked at him with a grin and carefully placed it in my pocket. I wasn't yet sure if I wanted to partake of it, or not.

Emerging Wisdom

For we write none other things unto you, that
what ye read or acknowledge; ...
– 2 Corinthians 1:13

We were traveling down the garden path once again. I hoped that we were getting closer to the light I was seeking. The fruitful insights I had gathered along the way were certainly making the journey more enjoyable.

My mind wandered over what I had gleaned to this point. I pondered the connection between the fruit of the tree of knowledge and how it played into the garden story. I was astounded by how much of the story contained unstated but profound insights which were shared between the lines. Thinking of this got me so stirred that I found myself bringing it up with my guide.

"It amazes me as to how much of the garden tale relies upon readers filling in the missing pieces of the story. Have you noticed this?"

"Absolutely!" is all that Sligh said.

"It amazes me that such a compact story has so much to say. Do you think this is what God had in mind when he inspired it?"

"That depends upon a lot of things."

"Like what?"

"Do you really think that these books within the Bible were written overnight, as if dictated by the voice of God for someone to record so that all could read it?"

I felt the trap of his words. He wanted me to acknowledge that the Bible was not something that had been dictated on just one occasion. He wanted me to disclose my best thoughts on the matter and at the moment I didn't feel up to it.

"Well?" he prodded me with an edgy impatient tone.

I had hesitated to respond, but just to get the conversation unstuck I replied, "I don't know."

"That's a great place to start," he said with an encouraging smile.

I was quite confused by his response to me. I thought he might be playing a one-upmanship game. There was a glimmer of hope though. His response showed all signs that he wanted to continue to work with me rather than against me.

"I suppose so," I said still cautious of a quick reversal. "I know that most all of these earlier books of the Bible were transmitted orally over many generations before they were finally written down. I guess I do know a bit more than I'd like to admit."

"Yes!" he said adding, "And just as within this conversation we're having now, as the story was handed down within each generation, there was a growing pearl of emerging wisdom within each communication."

"Wait a second," I interrupted. "Are you saying that the Bible didn't start out like it is written today?"

"What I'm saying is that no matter how sacred something is, when it is communicated, it is next to impossible to communicate orally without throwing in some of your own biases. That's the nature of oral communications."

"And each messenger will add his or her own bias to what is being communicated even after it has been written down," I threw in, hoping I was scoring points for contribution.

"Indeed. You can see this in the countless translations offered up to the altar of light." He smiled and went one step further with his thoughts on this. "And that's actually not necessarily a bad thing."

"Why do you say this?"

"By revealing the bias within each communication, there will be a greater tendency for feedback from the recipient of the communication. This feedback will help you recognize immediately whether what you added or adjusted was acceptable to your primary audience, or not."

I sat there in silence digesting what he had said. It made sense. I've used the same technique over the years whenever I've shared things with others. Conveying any idea successfully requires both a receptive audience and an effective way of encoding that idea so as to more readily communicate it. It must be written or presented so it will be understood in multiple ways and on multiple levels by multiple people for it to be successfully received and understood. The wrong words or the wrong order of presentation of the words can bring about a collapse of the bridge that carries the message over to the recipient.

"There's an added benefit," I said breaking the silence.

"What's that?"

"You can also tweak and add things each time once you find something that works to add value to the original idea."

"And if you do this over multiple tries and even multiple generations of messenger biases, you're bound to have a communication that is far superior to that which was initially conveyed. Eventually what is communicated, over several generations, is so masterful that it's as if God crafted it Himself."

"Are you saying that this is the case?"

"How could it not be the case? When the hand of God is involved, the inspiration to improve the value it conveys is inevitable."

"Do you mean to say that God is behind these improvements?"

"How could He possibly not be?" he replied. "In the beginning was the Word… and the Word was God."

I interrupted him, "Hold on! These communications are done through words. Is that what makes them God?"

"No. But the fact that they are superior words tells me that they were inspired by God."

"Is that how inspiration works?"

"Sometimes it does. With Words all things are possible."

"Oh, now you're just playing with me," I said rolling my eyes.

"In a way, *I am*," he admitted. "But the points I make are still valid."

"I can see that. Your word-play does have a feel of truth behind it and I can see the wisdom in your playfulness."

"Are you saying that you are seeing how God can be behind the inspiration of these books?" he said as he came back to the issue that got us into the conversation.

"I guess I am," I replied admitting that I had come to a firmer understanding. "I'm also seeing that sometimes things are not immediately obvious upon first glance."

"How's that?"

"My initial impression had been based upon a lack of insight and understanding. I didn't know what I didn't know."

"And now?"

"I have a different view from before. Talking it out and examining what was offered in a different light, I have concluded differently."

"That's how wisdom works. It's continually reviewing that which is before you, tweaking and adjusting it as you go, until it reveals the next level of understanding."

"I'm overwhelmed," was all that I could muster in response to all of this.

"Good! Profound insights take time to seep down into a solid foundation. You have much to think upon."

"Agreed," is all I could say. I had to stop there. All of this was a bit unnerving to hear. What he said rattled my way of looking at scripture. Could it be that I had had it all wrong? Was it possible that he was actually conveying something profoundly insightful and it was only now that I was realizing the treasure trove he was offering me?

Perfect

And the LORD God said, Behold, the man is become as one of us, to know good and evil: and now, lest he put forth his hand, and take also of the tree of life, and eat, and live for ever: – Genesis 3:22

We walked in silence for a little while, taking in the sights as we journeyed on toward the light. I went back to Sligh's comments about Adam and Eve's perfection. I mulled them over within my internal dialog. Unable to sort through it all, I broke the silence with, "I know we covered this, but I would like some further clarity."

"On what?" Sligh responded.

"Adam and Eve… were they perfect until they ate the fruit?"

"You ask that as if they were not perfect afterward."

"God's creation was perfect. It only became flawed when Adam and Eve sinned."

"In what way did it become flawed?"

"Death and disease… they didn't exist before Adam and Eve sinned."

"That's an assumption on your part. There's no proof of this. If anything, the story clearly tells us otherwise."

"It does not!" I retorted, disturbed that this had been turned around on me.

"I beg to differ with you, my friend," he replied, taking due care as to not increase my agitation.

"Where does it say otherwise?" I said almost demandingly.

"As before, your answer is in the midst of the garden."

"There are only two other important things in the midst of the garden; those two trees!"

"And those two trees are?" he asked with a musical tone.

"The tree of knowledge of good and evil and the tree of life!" I said quite firmly.

"Once again, the purpose of the second tree *is*?" he asked as if setting me up for a hopeful epiphany.

"Hmmm…," I sounded, considering the question carefully. This was the second time he asked me this question. Did I get it wrong the first time? Was he looking for a different response? What was his game?

He patiently waited for me to think it through. The effect of my next disclosure would echo throughout our continuing conversations so he knew I was painstakingly weighing my words. It took a while before I answered. The silence leading up to it was almost deafening.

Finally, taking a chance that he was merely looking for a confirmation of my last response, I said, "As we had discussed before, to enable you to live forever."

"Forever?"

"Yes. Forever… and before you say anything, let me just say that it's pretty clear from this that the tree had this purpose."

"And?"

"And I know where you're going with this," I said quickly.

"Oh! Where's that?"

"You're saying the tree of life provided fruit that when eaten provided immortality and that there would be no need for the tree if they were already immortal."

"So, as we had discussed, being created perfect does not mean that they were created to live forever?"

"Well," I interjected, "we can't know for sure because the story's pretty vague on a few things."

"On that, we can agree," he laughed. "And if we were to take the information presented at literal face value, the tree was there to offer immortality, regardless."

"Yes," I agreed, "it does appear that it was there for that very purpose. But couldn't it have been placed in the garden as a failsafe?"

"A failsafe?" he asked with a puzzled look.

"Yes, a failsafe inserted into God's creation just in case Adam and Eve fouled up their perfection."

"So, you're assuming that they were created immortal and messed that up. You believe that God knew they would mess their immortality up and so He put the tree of life in the garden before the fact so that they could still eat from it *when*, and not if, they messed up their immortality?"

"Exactly!"

"That's a bold assumption," I heard in a loving tone of voice coming from over on my left. I looked over and saw a young woman tending to an astonishing looking flower bed. Its mix of colors was a delight to the eyes.

"Hello, Sophie!" I heard Sligh say to her.

"Good morning, my good friend," she replied.

"This traveler is John," he pointed to me. "He's been seeking the light in the garden."

"And he made it past the burly cherubim unscathed?" she asked with a grin.

"Indeed!"

"Impressive," she said with an admirable tone.

Sligh looked over at Sophie and said, "Your arrival right now is most opportune, Sophie. Red will be coming back to get John soon, but right now I have to tend to a few things. Might you talk with John for a bit?"

Sophie looked at me and then back to Sligh. I didn't want to be a burden and was about to say that I can find my way when she said, "Sure, as long as we can continue the conversation you two were having. It sounds most interesting."

Sligh looked over at me and raised his eye-brow as if to say, "Your choice my friend." With a wave of his hand, he left.

I smiled and looked over at Sophie and asked, "How was it bold?"

"What?" she asked back.

"My assumption…"

She didn't let me finish and interrupted me with, "…Because if God knew they would screw up, then this story becomes a sick tale of a creator who set the whole thing up for Him to punish His creation."

I was startled by her statement. "Huh?"

"It has to do with free-will. If the conditions were set up so that there were no choices available to Adam and Eve, then God created them to fail which would have led to them getting punished through no fault of their own. If they actually had free-will, then it was their choices that drove the story forward."

"Wow! I had never considered that."

Free-Will

And the LORD God formed man of the dust of the ground, and breathed into his nostrils the breath of life; and man became a living soul. – Genesis 2:7

"But did Adam and Eve actually have free-will?" I asked with great interest.

"They would have to," she said without a second thought.

"You say that as if it were a fact."

"The story wouldn't make any sense if they didn't."

"Why do you say this?" I asked with interest.

"As I implied before, if they didn't have free-will, then God put them into the garden to fail."

"That's interesting! I had not thought of it in that way."

"That's why I stress that free-will *must* have been part of their make-up. Without it, the story would have been a sadistic tale of punishment for no good reason."

"Yikes! That makes so much sense once I think about it."

"Yes, and I have given it a lot of thought."

"When do you think free-will entered into them?"

"That's an interesting question. I imagine it occurred first with Adam."

"Why do you say this?"

"Because after God shaped the soil, the humus, into man to form the human Adam, He placed His Breath within His creation." [20]

"Are you telling me that God put His Spirit, and hence His Free-Will, into dirt to animate it?" I said in a surprised tone.

"I'm not telling you this; scripture is!"

"What do you mean?"

She looked at me, blinked and took a moment to collect her thoughts, and finally asked, "Do you remember what occurred right after God breathed into the shaped clay?"

"Yes. The man that He created became a living soul."

"I believe in that moment free-will was introduced into that creation."

"That's interesting! It's like a part of God was put within the clay in that moment."

"Like?" she interjected hoping I would understand what she was questioning.

"Oh!" I said thinking through what I had said, "Yes, not like, but in actuality, it would have had to be a part of God that was put into mankind."

"I agree," she assured me. "Since it was the Spirit of God that was put into the humus, then it would make sense that the Spirit's free-will would become part of that animated dirt as well."

"Is that your only evidence?"

"That's pretty much all of it. That is unless you want to look at how the story unfolds from there."

"Let's!" I exclaimed with eagerness to continue.

"Sure, what would you like to examine first?"

"How about the widely accepted belief that free-will can be commanded?"

"What do you mean?" she responded curiously.

Commanding

And the LORD God commanded the man, saying, Of every tree of the garden thou mayest freely eat: – Genesis 2:16

"Think about it. If you have free-will and another person has free-will, then you cannot command that the other free-will bend to yours."

"You mean, like by commanding the other to bend to your will, you're demanding that they give up their will in favor of yours?" Sophie asked.

"Exactly! The only thing that your free-will can hope for from the other free-will is that it chooses freely to cooperate and align with what you are asking. Otherwise commanding is a free-will negating action."

"That puts things in the garden into an irresolvable paradox then."

"You mean because God commanded Adam?"

"Yes!"

"I agree! One free-will cannot command another free-will without that other free-will giving up its free-will."

"But isn't that choice to give up one's free-will and go along with the command actually an *exercise* of free-will?"

"Yes. But only when that other free-will makes that choice freely."

"Freely?" she asked making effort to coax me into expanding my thoughts further.

100

"Yes. When a free-will is coerced into making a choice, then it's not an exercise of free-will."

"I disagree," she said sharing nothing further.

She could see that I expected more from her than the two words she had just offered. She was expecting me to pry into her statement... and then I saw the irony in what she was doing, so I laughed and gave in. "I have to pry, don't I?"

"You don't have to," she smiled. "But if you want more, you get to choose to go along with my implied invitation and ask, 'why.' It's your choice."

"I get it," I said finally. "No matter how you position yourself in the free-will game, you're still making a choice, even if you believe you have no other choice than to go along."

"And you don't *have to* go along."

"But that would mean you'd suffer the consequences from not going along."

"Yes. However, that's still a choice you have even when you believe you have no other choice that you like. The truth is, unless someone else is making the choice for you, you still have a choice."

"Let's put this thinking back into the garden scenario."

"Sure. Adam was commanded that he could freely eat of all the trees..."

"...but that's not a command!" I interrupted in protest. "I know that the word "command" is put there for us to accept it as a given, but the sentence doesn't make any sense."

"Meaning what?"

"It means that God informed Adam that he *may* do this. It's not a command. It's information! At best it's letting him know his options which, as I read it, are total."

"Indeed! And there's the problem that is in the way of understanding what was actually communicated."

"What's that?"

"Although the word used within the preserved writings has been most commonly translated as 'command', with a modern-day understanding of that word..."

"... are you going to tell me that scriptural scholars claim it says something different?" I blurted.

"Precisely!"

"But what do they claim it actually says?" I asked her, eager to have further light shed upon this interesting issue.

"More than one scholar says that the word that is translated to command was not meant to give Adam an order. It was meant to convey that God desired [21]Adam to know something."

"Like he was being given important information?"

"Exactly!" she replied.

"Wow! That makes far better sense to me than what others have told me it says."

"And coupling it with the other words within that sentence, it's clear that God was indeed letting Adam know what he could do."

"Are you referring to what God said that Adam *may freely do?*"

She nodded her head in affirmation adding, "And there's the *other* problem in truly understanding this."

I looked at her waiting for her to finish her thought but she didn't continue. It was obvious that she wanted me to ask and was leaving me with the tension of "there's more but you're going to have to ask to get it" hanging in the air. I bit at the bait, "Would you please expand upon that?"

She giggled. "Of course," she said with a smile. "If you take what follows that information [22] as a command as well, rather than as a caveat to what was shared, you're going to assume that Adam and Eve disobeyed."

"But didn't they?" I chimed in.

"Not if you take it as written."

"You mean *literally*?"

"Yes!"

"But it clearly says God commanded them not to eat!" I exclaimed.

"Does it?"

"I've been here before," I thought out loud trying to remind myself of previous conversations with others.

"Yes," she sighed. "Most people who have thought it through only thought they had, but they never had the insight of God's statements not being a command."

"Are you saying all three occurrences in the Garden story where God is reported to have used the word 'command' should be interpreted within the context of communicating information only?"

"Literature says this. And when you don't read what literature is telling you, you have left your understanding of

103

the story fully up to the influence of those who have read it and interpreted it *for you.*"

"So the Word needs to be understood within its context. Is that what you're saying?"

"Yes, and to do so in any other way is to understand it out of its context."

"So the word most commonly interpreted as 'command' may be an accurate translation, but it's a totally inappropriate interpretation?" I asked as my head started to spin with a mixture of confusion and excitement over the possibilities.

"Absolutely!" she fired back. "Take a look at that *camel* [23, 24] *going through an eye of a needle* [25] bit that ministers have been trying to explain for years."

"That never made any sense to me," I said in a soft personal tone.

"Of course it doesn't make sense to you!" she said. "The word that was translated to 'camel' is an accurate translation but a totally inappropriate interpretation."

"Wait! The translation is right but the interpretation is wrong?"

"Yes!"

"What would be a more accurate interpretation?"

"A thick rope or cable."

"How in the world did it become 'camel'?"

"Someone chose the wrong word in translating it. They had a possible choice of three words and they chose the wrong one."

"And as a result, there are generations of ministers making up things to try to make sense of a bad translation?"

"Yes. And because of this, people have had the wrong impression of what Yeshua was trying to convey through His offered lesson. And that same lesson applies to the word translated as *command* within these chapters of Genesis."

"So, it's the right translation; the wrong interpretation?"

"Spot on! Within the context of the story and the words used that surround the words, it can only mean that God was sharing information with Adam, important information that God desired him to know."

"Are you saying God *desired Adam to know* is a much closer translation than *command* based upon context?"

"What I'm saying is the surrounding text is saying this. Let's add it all up. You cannot command free-will. If we accept this as a fact, then the first statement God made is not a command but a conveyance from God of what Adam may do."

"It's not a command? It's only telling Adam what he has the liberty to do?"

"Yes. The statement that follows is a warning of what would occur if Adam actually *chose freely* to eat of one specific tree; it's not an order."

"Okay. I see that now. But what about the next time God is reported to have used the past tense of the word 'command'?"

"Commanded?" [26]

"Yes!"

"The same things apply. In the first incident, God was asking if Adam didn't heed his warning after God found out that Adam knew he was naked, which is an odd way to go about it since many believe that God knows everything."

"So, God actually asked a rhetorical question fully aware that He knew why Adam knew that he was naked?"

"Are you asking a rhetorical question here?" she giggled as she asked.

I stopped for a moment to reflect on our exchange and realized I had already answered my question. Of course, it was. God knew everything! "Then God's question was for Adam's benefit; not God's! Sort of like helping Adam realize both what he had done and why he was now aware that he was naked?"

"Again, with another rhetorical question?" she said with a Cheshire-cat smile.

"Good Lord, this is getting deep!" I exclaimed.

"Only as deep as you want to take it. God already knew. He was asking the question for Adam's benefit. Adam was going through some emerging awareness and wasn't yet connecting the dots between his choice and his new realizations."

"God was asking to help Adam along with this?"

"Again, with these rhetorical questions?" she grinned.

"Alright already," I said with a gasp of frustration. "It's clear that God was doing this for Adam's benefit. It appears from the story that Adam wasn't catching on to God's intent."

"Meaning what?"

"Well, for one, rather than just saying 'yes' and accepting the consequences for his choice, Adam started playing the blame game, giving every impression that he thought he had done something wrong rather than simply doing something that had a consequence."

"Agreed! And in the last instance of God using the past tense of command, the same thing applies."

"But in that instance, God says that he told Adam not to!" I stated in an effort to negate her argument.

"Unfortunately, if you take that slant, you'll have to also afford the serpent the same liberties."

"What liberties?" I asked, not understanding her addition of the serpent.

"By your measurement, God didn't include the warning He gave the first time. Hence, God didn't tell the whole truth this time. Well, the serpent didn't speak the whole truth either."

"What do you mean?" I demanded.

"The first time God warned Adam not to eat the fruit and told him that there would be consequences if he did. Yet, in His last use of the past tense of the word *command*, God said that He told Adam not to eat from the tree and didn't repeat the 'or there will be consequences' part of His original warning. But because that part was left out, it leaves readers with the impression that God had instituted a prohibition rather than merely reaffirming a warning of consequences."

"Wow! No wonder this has been misunderstood for so many years. The right translation of the word was put forth in the story with the wrong interpretation. This has wrought havoc upon generations."

"And as a result, generations have thought that Adam and Eve disobeyed a command rather than realizing they were simply trying to dismiss any accountability for their choices."

Shifting the Blame

And the man said, The woman whom thou gavest
to be with me, she gave me of the tree, and I did
eat. And the LORD God said unto the woman,
What is this that thou hast done? And the woman
said, The serpent beguiled me, and I did eat.
– Genesis 3:12-13

Red stuck his head out from behind some bushes and coughed playfully to break my concentration; it worked. I stopped my conversation with Sophie and looked up at him, waiting for his next words. He gave me a boyish grin; one that would precede some playful banter.

He asked, "What are you two so gosh darn focused upon?"

"We've been talking about Eden stuff," Sophie replied.

"Ah! Still talking 'bout Adam and Eve's disobedience, are we?" he teased.

"Not really," I muttered. "We were discussing free-will and how it can't be commanded."

"So that means they didn't disobey?" he asked, prodding me into playing along and commenting.

I was not expecting such a quick shift in focus. Red saw this in my eyes as I stammered to say something as my thoughts were forming. "Wait... They most certainly disobeyed. That's what's been taught from the beginning. Adam and Eve disobeyed God's command," I put it out there hoping it would help gel my thoughts.

"My work is done here, fellas," Sophie interrupted us. "I

have to get to another section of the garden. It was nice meeting you, John," she said as she gathered her tools.

"Thanks for the enlightening chat," I responded.

"You're most welcome, John," Sophie said as she took off for her next garden destination.

"Well, it's not about any perceived disobedience John," Red went into it, not allowing Sophie's exit to derail the train of thought. "It has more to do with their trying to shift the blame for their choices," he said as he stepped from behind the bushes and sat down caddy-corner on the rocks before me.

"What do you mean?" I asked.

"Haven't you read the report?" he motioned to his backpack where he kept his Bible.

"Well, sure I have!" I exclaimed leaning over and tapping at his backpack.

"Then where is it in the report that our friends start shifting the blame?"

"You're going to make me think about it, aren't you?" I said facetiously.

"Well, of course," he said with a smile. "It wouldn't be a good conversation without some thinking thrown in, would it? You still have some time for some of that don't you?"

"Yes, I do," I said with a forced sigh. "Okay, I'll bite."

"Good!" he replied getting up, giving me a two-thumbs-up sign and motioning me to follow him further down the trail. I followed his lead.

"As I recall the report, the first volley, I mean, *blaming incident* occurred was when God asked Adam what he had done."

"Yes, and then what happened?"

"Adam really didn't admit to doing anything until he pointed his finger at Eve."

"What was the implication?"

"That even though Adam ate the fruit, he was implying that it wasn't his fault."

"Why implied?" he pried, hoping I would say it for him.

"Well, when you really think about what Adam was doing, he was pointing the finger at Eve and indirectly claiming that it was not his fault that he ate the fruit…"

"Implying what?"

"That Adam was blaming Eve for his eating the fruit," I said as a matter of fact.

"I agree with your assessment, John," he said firmly and added, "but that's not the only one who Adam was blaming."

"Huh?" I said with a bit of surprise.

"In your mind, reread the words Adam used to convey to God his innocence."

"Ah! Okay… I get it," I said in a focused tone.

"Get what?"

"Are you claiming that Adam indirectly accused God!"

"What are you implying?"

"When Adam responded to God's question, he referred to God as having given the woman to him."

"And what are the implications of this addition to Adam's response?" he pressed.

"The central implication is that Adam insinuated in his reply that if God had not put the woman in Adam's life to temp him, Adam would not have had the opportunity to eat the fruit'"

"I agree with your assessment. Is there more"

"Yes. That would also mean that Adam was not only blaming Eve for his actions, he was also implicating God as being at fault for putting her into his life!"

Red let out a sigh of satisfaction. He saw that I had gotten it! Or at least I voiced the connections. He didn't let up on me though. "What is reported to have happened next, John?"

"If I recall scripture correctly, God asked Eve what she had done."

"Yes, but if you look at how God asked, it was an open ended question," he pointed out.

"Please explain this if you would."

"Okay. Was God asking about her tempting Adam with the Fruit or was God asking about her eating the fruit?"

"Great question Red," I said giving the question further thought. "It's pretty clear that she responded as if God were asking about her eating the fruit."

"Yes, almost negating Adam's blaming her by shifting the focus from being blamed to blaming the serpent…"

"Indeed!" I interjected. "And there's a further implication in Eve's statement."

"What?"

"Well, one thing is for sure," I said pausing to get my attention focused, "God put the serpent in the garden as well!"

"Ah!" he exclaimed with glee. "So, if God had not put the serpent into the garden, Eve would not have been deceived into eating the fruit!"

"Exactly! Eve responded even more slightly than Adam did in implicating God in her choice."

"So, they both made efforts to shift the blame from themselves and indirectly accused God of being to blame for their choices."

"Yeah, they sure did think that they had put one over on God.

"As do most people who try to shift the accountability for their choices over to others," Red said in a tone that revealed to me a deeply felt sadness.

The Insidious Plot

> *And unto Adam he said, Because thou hast*
> *hearkened unto the voice of thy wife, ...*
> *– Genesis 3:17*

"It's pretty insidious when you think about it," he blurted.

"What's that?" I asked, trying to figure out where Red was going with our conversation.

"The blame shifting game that Adam and Eve were trying to play on God."

"Ah!" I said adding nothing while I waited for more from him.

He waited a few seconds before he spoke. "You're not asking me the obvious," he piped up breaking the silence.

"Yes," I said with a smile, "I figured you'd let me know when you couldn't hold it in any longer."

We laughed. I saw the game that we were playing with each other. One of us would cast something out to bait the other, hoping the bait would be taken and acted upon before the caster had to reel it in to re-bait the hook.

"Okay, I'll *say* the obvious."

"Good!" I said in relief. "I was about to burst."

He smiled and added, "We both recognize that Adam and Eve were deliberately trying to shift the blame for their choices."

"Yes," I affirmed. "It's clear from the book that they were pointing their fingers at others and not themselves."

113

"But they were also doing something else in that pointing," he said letting the statement hang, fully aware that I knew there was more to come.

"Okay!" I said dramatically adding, "I give up! Please! Let me in on your insight."

"I'm glad you're interested," he said with a giggle. "Adam and Eve wanted someone else to pay for their choice."

"Hmmm…," is all that I responded with. I knew this was occurring but I had never had it voiced like this to me before. "Payment… I don't think I have ever had that said to me before about Adam and Eve."

"Never?" he asked almost in disbelief.

"I've talked with a lot of people about this story and I don't remember anyone of them connecting Adam and Eve trying to outrun their accountability with trying to get someone else to pay for their choices."

"Hence the term *insidious*," he said as a tieback to his original statement.

"I'm seeing it now," I said thoughtfully. "If they could get someone else to accept or take the blame, then the next logical step would be to load the consequences for the choice upon the target…"

"…much like one would do to a scapegoat?"

"Yikes!" I exclaimed. "And just like the original scapegoat in the Good Book carries off the sins of those who load it up, the target for the blame becomes the individual who pays for the sins; not the actual person who made the choice to sin."

He looked at me and said the following, "Are you saying that Adam and Eve were fully willing to allow another

114

individual to suffer the consequences for their choices rather than step forward themselves and own them?"

I sat there in silence. The ramifications of his question spread like a firework blast in the sky of my mind, expanding outward illuminating everything in its path and more.

But something didn't sit right with the analogy. I knew scapegoat lore. Scapegoats came in pairs. One of them was always offered up as a blood sacrifice to God. The other was symbolically loaded up with the sins in question and driven off into the wilderness. Both were innocent, or at least, *not guilty;* only one got slaughtered initially. Later scriptures and rabbinical writings indicated the one that was driven out into the wilderness eventually was thrown off a cliff.

The same thing came to my mind though; these creatures were innocent and they suffered deliberately so that the guilty parties didn't have to. Nowadays, *scapegoat* is a term that means that an innocent had been blamed for and saddled with something they didn't do and that this innocent was going to be made to suffer for something for which they were not truly responsible for. In the case of Adam and Eve, they were making every effort to have someone else suffer for accountability that they didn't want to accept.

"What are you pondering John?" Red asked interrupting my flow of thought. "You appear to be deep into something."

"I'm making some connections with what you shared."

"And?"

"Adam blamed both Eve and God and, by default, he was implying that they should be judged responsible for his choice and held accountable for any consequence that would naturally follow."

"Yes. Eve did similar with the serpent and with God by association."

"I'm seeing that as well," I said showing great discomfort.

"What's troubling you?"

"I see this behavior all the time," I responded sadly.

"People blaming Eve, the serpent and God?" he quipped.

I chuckled. "No, silly," I said laughingly. "I see people trying to outrun their accountability for their choices and blaming others for their life conditions. It's pandemic! From their vantage point, they are *never* to blame and they are *perpetual* victims."

"Oh, it's worse than that. The people who believe them support that victim's view and boldly attack anyone who would dare contest it. So, the offending parties are never

held to account by those with like minds who surround them."

"Do you think the story was a warning to mankind?"

"The story? You mean the story of Eden's garden?"

"Yes."

"No, John," he said with sincere conviction. "It was not a warning. "

"Then what was it?"

"It was a *description*."

My mind exploded with connections. "Wait!" I blurted, "Are you saying that mankind as a whole does this?"

"That is exactly what I am saying," he responded without skipping a beat. "The book merely describes what humans have been doing from the beginning."

"You've given me much to think over, Red."

"Good!" he said with gusto. "Come, let us continue down the path and move closer to that light you seek. Are you up for some refreshment?"

"You mean food and drink?"

"But of course."

"I guess I could go for some."

"Great! There's a snack bar up ahead."

"Your garden has a snack bar?" I said in disbelief.

"Don't *all* good gardens?" he replied with a wink.

Part III

The Exile

When the whistle blows,
everyone gets out of the pool.

Arrogance

*For by thy words thou shalt be justified,
and by thy words thou shalt be condemned.*
– Matthew 12:37

We came upon the snack bar soon enough. It had an enchanting layout with tables positioned under awnings made of actual live plants. The sign over the counter had a nice assortment on its menu right under the calligraphy letters spelling out, "Garden Club Café." It was quite impressive for a snack bar.

"Good morning!" I heard a voice say coming from behind the counter. I looked over and couldn't see who was speaking. The voice continued though with, "Have a seat gentleman. I'll be right over."

We meandered through the tabled area and found ourselves sitting about twenty feet from the counter. Soon thereafter we were approached by one of the snack bar workers. "What'll it be gentlemen?"

I knew what I wanted. I had already eyed the menu hanging over the snack bar counter. "I'm in the mood for one of your fruit slurries. I'll take the mix," I said.

"I'll take the same to go," Red said.

I looked over at Red as if to say, "where ya goin'?"

"Yeah," he interjected knowing full well what I had said indirectly. "I know. I'll be back soon enough. Enjoy your slurry," he said, motioning over to the server, "it's on me."

Before I could object to his offer, the server stopped me with a nudge to my shoulder. "What's your name there, chap?" she said as she interrupted my focus on Red leaving so soon.

"Oh, where are my manners," Red said in an embarrassed tone. "Dawn, this is John. He's seeking the light in the garden."

"And he made it past the burly cherubim?"

"He sure did and without losing any limbs!"

They both laughed, and I began to feel like there was an inside joke going on between all those I encountered in this garden.

"Glad to meet you, John," Dawn said and held out her hand.

"Same here," I said, shaking her hand while feeling a bit disoriented by all the swift exchanges.

"We've been walking toward the light in the garden and talking about Adam and Eve stuff," Red said.

"Yes," I added. "We've just about got the original sin pegged down."

"Ah! Arrogance…" she said trailing off in thought and then motioned the other server behind the counter as to what we had ordered.

"Wait! Arrogance?" I repeated in confusion, not too sure I understood the connection.

"Yes," she affirmed. "It's the actual original sin that Adam and Eve were guilty of committing within the garden."

"I'd never considered that angle," I confessed. "I suppose it could be said that arrogance was behind the sin, but I can't
120

see that it actually was the sin," I confessed. "Isn't arrogance a quality rather than a sin?"

"It's a foundation," she said as a matter-of-fact.

"Interesting... arrogance is defined as having or revealing an exaggerated sense of one's own importance or abilities. How is that sinful?"

"Does it not describe an aspect of falling short?"

"I see where you're getting your conclusion."

"Good! Their choices in the garden revealed their true character."

"Was it their choice to eat the fruit that revealed this?"

"Not at all. Eating the fruit was inspired by a desire to gain knowledge, most often taken to be wisdom. That's not in the least bit an arrogant action nor is it motivated by arrogance.

"Are you saying that their arrogance was revealed only afterward?"

"Not directly. However, it's implied by what is shared."

"What exactly did they do afterward that was arrogant?"

"Just a second," she said as she went over to the counter to get our order. She returned smiling, "I think you'll like these. They're made from our garden fruits." She handed the slurries to Red and me.

"Thanks! Enjoy your chat with Dawn my friend," Red said to me as he headed out. "I'll be back soon!"

Dawn was quick to bring me back to the topic. "So, let's get back to your question about what they did. They chose to try to break with reality believing they had the power to do so."

"Break with reality? Power to do so?" I asked in confusion. "What on earth are you saying?"

"When there were asked what they had done, they didn't own it until they had first discounted their ownership by blaming others."

"But they did still own it."

"Yes, and with the caveat that implied that they were not at fault."

"Where's the arrogance in that?"

"Think it through with me, John. What makes a person arrogant is thinking that they were so important that they could discount or ignore their choices and actions by exaggerating how little their choices contributed to the outcome, especially when their whole focus was on making efforts to discount the relevance of their choice in favor of who influenced who in making their choice."

All I could say at that moment was, "That's a whole lot to digest."

Dawn smiled in agreement. "There's a lot going on in that story that many readers don't take the time to study. If they did, they might come to a better understanding as to why their own lives are often so messed up when they continue to behave the same way."

"Are you saying that people routinely dismiss how their own choices make their lives the way that they are?"

"Yes. But I'm not stopping there. I'm saying people routinely point toward *others* as the reason they made their choices. This implies that these *others* are to blame first, for the choices that were made, because of the influence on them from those *others*. Secondly, those *others* are at fault for having *influenced them* into making the choices they made. The further implication is that, due to that fault, these *others* are to be held to account for the outcome, the consequences, rather than the person who made the choices.

"That means the life being lived by the blamer, the one passing the blame, is a life where he or she chooses to see himself or herself as a victim of outside influences."

"Yes," she replied adding, "and being a victim of outside influences means that the blamers are also saying that they are not in control of what occurs in their life..."

I interrupted her, "I can see where this is going."

"Where's that?"

"If they are not in control, then they can't truly affect or make change."

"Which means what?"

"In their belief system, they cannot be the ones who rescue themselves from the lives they created by their choices."

"Sadly, I have to agree. However, there's arrogance underlying in all this."

"I'm not seeing it. What are you seeing that I am not?"

"They're operating on the belief that their choices don't cause situations in their life," she started to explain.

"So?"

She looked at me and paused. "John, they believe that their choices don't cause their lives and they don't realize that that is still a choice!"

"Huh?" I half spoke in utter confusion.

"They have chosen to redirect the responsibility for their choices. In one breath they are saying their choices don't matter and, in another breath, they are choosing to point the finger at others as if that choice does matter."

"So, on one hand, these blamers are saying that no one should put any weight of importance on the choices they make because each choice was based upon outside influences. On the other hand, they are directing others to place great weight on their choice to blame outside influences for the choices they themselves made."

"Exactly! You cannot have it both ways."

"I'm seeing that they are choosing to not be held to account for their choices."

"Now you're getting the gist of why this is arrogance incarnate. The rules are simple. *Your* choices affect *your* life. You cannot believe that you can choose to not have your choices affect your life without being arrogant. *The Rule of Choices* applies to everyone without exception!"

"You mean that the rules apply even if you claim that they don't?"

"Yes. Choosers can't choose to have the choosing rules changed just because they choose to believe another choice makes them safe from previous choices. Those who try to do this are displaying arrogance."

Her words overwhelmed me. It took some time for me to digest them. She gave me time to reflect upon them though and I was grateful that she did. When my thoughts and feelings finally settled down, I asked, "Are you saying Adam and Eve were arrogant because they believed they were trying to choose to not be held to account for their choices?"

"That's exactly what I'm saying," she said nodding her head in slow assurance. "In every case, the moment you believe you should not be affected by your choices is the moment you're acting arrogantly."

"And this is what Adam and Eve did in the garden?"

"It is!"

"But they simply answered God's question," I protested.

"Yes. They did indeed. And both responses appear to be straightforward and direct. That is, until you examine them both for their implications."

"Implications?"

"Yes. It's clear from how God responded to them that He realized they were trying to shift the blame."

"I don't understand…"

"If they had simply responded that they ate the fruit, they would have been communicating that they had chosen to own their choice."

"Ah! But they first pointed their fingers at others before they fessed up…"

"You got it!" she interrupted. "And God realized this and let them know what would occur when they tried to outrun their accountability for the choices they made."

"You mean when God said, 'because you did this' was not about eating the fruit?"

"It wasn't at all about eating the fruit."

"No?" I responded in a bit of confusion. "What was it about?"

"It was about how they tried to dismiss ownership of their choice to eat it by blaming others for that choice."

It took a moment for what she said to settle in. The connections were being made like a series of dominos falling one upon another. They believed *the rule of choices* didn't apply to them. Was this arrogance or simply a matter of ignorance as to how the universe operates?

As I was about to ask, Red showed up and interrupted our discussion. As he did, Dawn motioned to me that there were some newly arriving customers and that she had to get back to work.

We would have to continue our conversation at another time.

126

Banishment

*"Therefore the LORD God sent him forth from the
garden of Eden, to till the ground from whence he
was taken. So he drove out the man; ..."*
– Genesis 3:23-24

Dawn's comments echoed in my mind as Red and I continued toward the garden's light. As I sojourned in the garden, I began to have an entirely different appreciation for the scriptures of my youth. Everyone I encountered added to that appreciation and I was looking forward to more of the same.

One thing did come to mind though. What was the reason as to why Adam and Eve were kicked out of the garden? If they didn't disobey God's commandment, could it be their arrogance? If that were the reason, then why couldn't God have simply dealt with that issue *within* the garden?

I decided to bring up this question with Red. "Why do you think it was so important for God to exile Adam and Eve from the garden?" I asked.

"I can take three entirely different directions with your question. Which one would you like to take first?"

"I don't know these directions so I can't answer your question."

"Actually, you do," he said with a smile. "You've already hinted at them."

"I have?" I said quite in disbelief.

"Yes. You hinted at it when you said they chose not to be held accountable for their choices."

"Ah! You overheard my conversation with Dawn?"

"Yes, but just the part that I heard as I approached."

"So, that's only one. What are the other two?"

"You hinted at the second when you said God didn't want them to eat from the tree of life, especially after eating from the tree of knowledge, and you hinted at the third when you said that they were seeing things differently."

"Wow!" I exclaimed. "You've been keeping track of all this?"

"Of course I have. What you share with me is important.

"I guess it was. At least what you just put back in my lap."

"Well, you did ask me why they were exiled, didn't you?"

"Yeah!" I laugh realizing my new found friend had been listening and not losing any of it. "I did indeed."

"I think that all three are relevant though."

"I sense they are all somehow interconnected."

"They are," he responded adding, "and in ways that require careful analysis."

"Let's cover the first," I suggested.

"Okay. How about discerning what the outcome of the first: *choosing to not be accountable for their choice.* What would this choice have brought about?"

"I think you'd have a lot of people pointing fingers at everyone else. The blaming of others would be the only game in town."

"And with enough choices being made with no one wanting to accept accountability for them, utter chaos would ensue."

"Without ownership, the garden would quickly have become a mess with each choice that was made and no one would be stepping up to claim ownership of any of them."

"You're not painting a pretty picture of Paradise."

"It wouldn't be a pretty sight. Everyone would be making choices and every last one of those making choices would be outrunning accountability by choosing not to be held accountable for their previous choices."

"Sort of like things are now in some people's lives?" he asked bringing the focus back on life.

"Exactly! As I said before, I see this occur all too often."

"As do I," he related. "The intimate connection between making a choice and having an outcome is that the outcome is a direct result of the choice and how that choice is supported by its environment."

"In Adam and Eve's case, they chose to eat the fruit. That's clearly apparent by what is reported."

"Is there something that's *not* clearly reported?"

"Yes. When they were questioned about eating the fruit, rather than simply saying, 'yes' that they had eaten it, they first discounted their choice to eat it by claiming that their choice was driven by someone else's influence."

"And this choice of action did what?" he asked.

"It discounted their respective responsibilities for their own individual choices. Furthermore, if they had been successful, it would have shifted the responsibility for their choice to the shoulders of others so that those others, instead of the original choice-maker, would then be held to account for the choice that was made."

"Pretty convoluted, eh?"

"I'll say! They blamed their choice to eat the fruit on others. And they did it to shift the focus off of the fact that it was *their* choice and put that focus onto others."

"This is exactly what occurred. And the way that the book is written leads readers to believe that God punished the serpent, then Eve and then Adam for the influence that each had upon the other."

"Agreed!" I exclaimed. "And then we are led to believe that Eve was punished for listening to the serpent and Adam for listening to Eve."

"So, it was a two-way punishment?"

"Of course, Adam and Eve thought that they were being punished for being influenced and Eve and the serpent were being punished for being influencers."

"Everyone was punished in some way except for God."

"But God was certainly the one perceived to be doling out the punishment."

"If you do not want to take credit for your choices, someone has to," he said with a wink.

"But that's the challenge in understanding all this."

"What is?"

"When you examine closely everything that was taken as a punishment from God, every one of the consequences stated were natural consequences of living life, for their choice to not take responsibility for their choices, and for blaming others for the life they chose to live when they made those choices," I stated.

"Eve's sorrow, pain, desires, and being ruled over?" [27] he asked.

"Yes! All due to not accepting her responsibility for the choices she made."

"You mean Adam's toil, being bound to the land that provides both pain and sustenance?" [28]

"No. For Adam's blaming of his wife for his choice and not accepting his personal responsibility." [29]

"You make it sound like their view of what life was going to offer to them was as a punishment rather than as a blessing," he said facetiously.

"When you blame others for what you have created in your life, you view yourself as being put upon, or being victimized, by others rather than as you being your life's steward and getting to make choices for yourself. And that covers the third item that you mentioned earlier."

"Ah! As a result of them choosing to not accept accountability for their choices, their whole world-view was that they were victims of the influence and choices of others."

"Yes," I agreed. "The outcomes of life events caused by their choices were being done *to them* rather than *by them*."

"Views naturally embraced by those who deny that their choices have anything to do with the life they have as a result of those choices."

"You mentioned, too, that God didn't want them to eat from the tree of life," I said returning to the second thing he mentioned.

"Yes. God saw that man had become like 'one of Us' to know good and evil."

131

I finished what he had started, "…and lest man reach out and eat from the tree of life and therefore live forever… God blew the whistle and told everyone to get out of the pool."

"He did not," he said not realizing I was pulling his leg.

"He might as well have," I laughed. "God kicked those two kids out of the garden as soon as they had become like Him, at least as far as knowing good and evil."

"But was it because they now knew good and evil or was it for an entirely different reason?"

"If you ask the typical person on the street, they would say they were kicked out because they disobeyed God's commandment."

"But that's not what scripture says was the reason," he insisted. "You just said the reason for His having blown the whistle. What was it really?

"Scriptures say that He didn't want them to reach out to eat from the tree of life…"

He interrupted me and asked, "Yes, but why?"

"To eat its fruit and therefore live forever?" I said in a half questioning tone.

"Exactly!" he said with vigor. "Why do you suppose God wouldn't want His creation to live forever?"

"I'm sensing that it has to do with the other two things we covered?" I asked and by doing so answered my own question.

He smiled seeing that I had already made the connection. "Of course, they are the reasons. Adam and Eve were not just being irresponsible. They were also blind as to how they were causing their lives to unfold by the choices they were making."

"No wonder God kicked them out. If they had eaten from the tree of life, they would have been in the garden forever, continuing to always make a mess of things and blaming everyone else for their choices."

"That's only half right."

"Which half was right?" I asked trying to figure out which portion of my statement was hitting the mark.

"The part about those irresponsible kids living forever and making a mess of things."

"So, which part was not right?" I asked with confusion.

"The part about God kicking them out."

"Wait? Are you saying that God didn't force them out of the garden?"

"Yes, I am."

"But that's not what's reported!"

"If you take it literally, you'll believe that God was the one driving the man out."

"You mean there's more to it than just reading it literally?"

"Are all the things that occurred to Adam and Eve natural consequences or not?"

"Wait! Are you saying that they kicked themselves out, believing it was God directing them?"

"If you choose to believe life consequences are always being done *to you* rather than being a direct result of your choices, you're going to experience everything that occurs to you as if it was someone doing something *to you.* Furthermore, your narrative will drip with blame for everyone except yourself. You'll never accept that your choices are what drove your life in the direction it's taking."

"Are you claiming those who wrote the scripture were trying to capture the viewpoint of Adam and Eve when they wrote the story down?"

"How can it not be any other way? Clearly we're told that the kingdom of God is within us." [30, 31]

"But Eden is not the kingdom of God!" I exclaimed, not wanting to believe the two were in any way connected.

"How could it not be?" Red asked with a smile. "Isn't it all about how one wants to perceive things?

I had to think about it. By direct implication, he was saying that Adam and Eve never left the garden. Because of the choices they had made for their lives they had come to *believe* that they did leave. But how did this come to occur? I experienced a flood of thoughts making their way through my mind. I finally spoke up and asked, "The story hinges more on how Adam and Eve perceived their situation rather than on what had actually occurred?"

"Yes. Because of the choices they had made Adam and Eve saw things differently and, as a result, the story is revealed through their eyes. That's what makes it such a confusing report."

Through Their Eyes

So he said, "I heard Your voice in the garden,
and I was afraid because I was naked;
and I hid myself." – Genesis 3:10

"But how exactly did Adam and Eve see things differently?" I asked.

"That's a great question to ask!" Red said. "Do you remember earlier on how the story said that they were naked and that they were unashamed?"

"Yes, I do."

"Do you remember how shortly after they ate the fruit that they saw that they were naked and they were afraid?"

"Wait! I remember reading this. That's interesting…"

"What's interesting?" he asked, hoping that I would make the connection.

"Well," I paused to search for the right words, "they were naked and unashamed before they ate, and then *afterward they saw that they were naked.* It's almost like they didn't realize that they were naked prior to eating the fruit. Or at least, it didn't matter to them if they were."

"Almost like, or was it that they truly didn't realize what nakedness was or what it meant and what the ramification of this state had to do with their safety?" he put forth trying to stress an important point.

"The latter would hold more weight for me Red," I said with a firm tone. "It fits nicely into my last statement. They certainly had a transformation in their awareness when they

135

partook of that fruit and that changed how they saw themselves in relation to their environment."

"I agree. That shift in awareness did something more."

"What's that?"

"They experienced authentic emotion for the first time, but only after they ate the fruit."

"You know," I spoke thoughtfully. "I hadn't looked into that aspect before."

"No?"

"Not once!" I confessed. "Nowhere before their eating did they show any indication of emotion."

"Even when Adam said 'At last!' to God when Eve was created?"

"Yes, even then. Anyone can read emotion into the statement and get away with it. However, that's an interpretation that doesn't fit with what was stated later just before they ate the fruit."

"What's that?"

"You said it before," I reminded him, "they were naked and unashamed. That shows a total lack of emotion, Red. It can't get any clearer than that."

"Alright, I'll have to concede to you on this point that the story really doesn't reveal any discernibly legitimate emotional states prior to their eating the fruit."

"Thanks," I said happy to state a point that he already had concluded.

"But what about after they had eaten the fruit?"

"Later on? Do you mean when God started questioning them about what they did?"

"Yes. More like immediately after they ate the fruit, God asked where Adam was."

"And Adam said that he was afraid so he hid."

"Exactly!" That was definitely an emotional response."

"Agreed!" Are there other examples?"

"Yes," he said. "Remember what God said to Eve when He was telling her about the consequences of her action, about how she would experience bearing children?"

"Yes."

"Why did God specifically say that Eve would bring forth children in emotional pain?"

"Emotional pain? I don't remember ever reading that before. Where does it say this?"

"It's in Genesis 3:16," Red said, adding, "To the woman He said, I will greatly multiply your grief and your suffering in pregnancy and the pangs of childbearing; with spasms of distress you will bring forth children."

"Are you saying that it implies that Eve was going to experience these emotions as a result of her raising her kids and not just giving birth?"

"I'm saying scripture is communicating this. I'm merely letting you know what it says."

Red had an uncanny way of making his points. I had to agree. The emotional aspect of Adam and Eve's lives sure did open up once they ate the fruit. "But all of this sounds like God is doing this to them."

"Yep. And from the point of view of Adam and Eve, it is being done to them. But when you look at what is being said, they are merely experiencing life as victims…"

"…and the story conveys this through victim's eyes," I added.

"That's for sure! And this victim view is being expressed by the writers to drive that point home."

"Wait! The writers were purposefully expressing Adam and Eve's experience this way?"

"Indeed! And until you understand this, you'll never see through the veil that has been placed over the tale. But that's getting away from the focus…"

"The emotions," I said, interrupting him.

"Yes. There's a clear demarcation between how they experienced life before partaking of the fruit and life after it."

"What do you mean?"

"Prior to it, they did not truly perceive much about what was before them."

"And what occurred afterward?"

"After they partook, they saw life through the eyes of knowing beings; albeit, with limited knowledge, but they had become able to make new connections with what they now saw, connections that only knowledge would create."

"As in, connecting the vision of a lack of clothes with what it is to be naked, and the ramifications of that state?"

"Yes," he replied adding, "and the emotional pain that would naturally occur when raising offspring."

Inheritance

Direct my footsteps according to your word;
let no sin rule over me. – Psalm 119:133 NIV

"But what about this original sin claim?" I asked curious as to what he might share with me.

"What about it?" Red responded without going into actually answering my question.

"Is the original sin transferable?" I questioned him more assertively.

"The actual sin or the propensity to sin?" he asked me back instead of playing into my question.

"The actual sin," I answered hoping he would have some insights into what I was seeking.

"I'm informed that it is not transferable," he said without elaborating any further.

He must have sensed that I wanted more though he didn't offer anything further. I knew from his look that I would have to probe further for he wasn't volunteering any more light on the matter.

"How were you informed of this?" I half-demanded.

"The Good Book," he said pointing once again to the Bible he had in his back-pack. To my surprise, he reached over to it, pulled it out, handed it over to me, and pointed to the yellow bookmark at the top. "Go ahead, open it up and read the highlighted section."

Without hesitation I did as he requested, carefully opening up to the bookmarked page and I sought with my eyes the highlighted areas he mentioned. There the section was, *Deuteronomy 24:16,* toward the center of the left page. It read as follows:

"Fathers shall not be put to death for their sons,
nor shall sons be put to death for their fathers;
everyone shall be put to death for his own sin."

As I read through it, he gently directed my attention to another section saying, "And before you comment, especially about the verse sounding like you will be put to death for sinning, please read this section as well."

I followed his finger. It pointed to another bookmarked section, Ezekiel 18:20, and I read that too.

"The person who sins [is the one that] will die.
The son will not bear the punishment for the sin of the
father, nor will the father bear the punishment for the
sin of the son; the righteousness of the righteous shall
be on himself, and the wickedness of the wicked shall
be on himself."

I read it through and as my eyes showed that I had completed the passage, Red asked, "Does that answer both of your questions."

"Actually, all it says is that you're not punished or put to death for the sins of anybody else. But it doesn't really say whether or not the sin of one person is transferred to anybody else."

"If it were transferrable, what evidence would you have to see so you'd know?"

"I hadn't given it that much thought Red," I responded though I felt a bit stupid for not thinking it through.

"The first scripture you read says people who sin are put to death for their own sins."

"So?"

"According to this scripture, you shouldn't be put to death for the sin of another."

"Oh!" I said, finally making the connection. "So, only Adam and Eve could be put to death, or punished, for their own sins."

"Your statement speaks a truth that far too many people do not realize."

"But, if we couple that with the second scripture, does that mean none of their offspring should be punished for their sins as well?"

"It's pretty straight forward and when you think about it, people have enough shortcomings of their own to begin with. They don't need to be taking upon themselves the sins of others to have something to feel guilty about."

We laughed. We knew all-to-well the truth that had been just spoken.

"What about the claim that we inherited the propensity to sin?" I asked.

"As in, it's in our moral genetic makeup?"

"Yes," I said and paused in thought.

"What's going on in that head of yours?"

"Well," I said with hesitation. "It's clear that there is an agenda being pushed by specific groups to have us buy into the idea that all mankind have been stained by the sin of Adam and Eve."

"Ah! That whole doctrine of the original sin!"

"Yes!"

"It isn't supported by scripture."

"But I was told that scripture does back it up."

"Yes. I'm sure there are a lot of people in various institutions who bank on you believing that innocent children need to be washed to cleanse them of some imaginary original sins. But we just went over that. Isn't it clear from what is written that inheriting sin is just bogus?"

"I'd have to agree," I said. "However, I can see something more in this."

"What's that?"

"That by being created without any previous knowledge children will naturally have a tendency to engage in wishful thinking."

"What does that mean for people in general?"

"Until they experience enough of life to know better, they are apt to believe that they can outrun their choices and the consequences of those choices."

"So, are you saying that the idea of original sin is a natural consequence of God having created us as uninformed choice-makers who must learn as we go?"

"I'm saying far more than that. Human beings make choices believing that they have the power to allow themselves to outrun their accountability and until they are surrounded by people and conditions that teach them otherwise, they will continue in that sinful state."

"And people in this state of being would make a mess of God's garden if allowed to continue unchecked?" he asked.

"Yes, and they would do so without fail!"

"Is it any small wonder that Adam and Eve believed they were no longer in the garden?"

"Considering they would experience a tsunami of consequences within a very short time that would carry them down a landslide of woe, they would very naturally perceive they were no longer in a land of bliss."

"You say that as if you have experienced this first hand."

"Yes, and more than once. And I can tell you without reservation that I wanted to blame everyone but myself for the conditions that I created."

"Did you?" Red asked.

"At first I did."

"Then what happened?"

"I realized how much of my life I had caused, all by myself, and there was no one other than myself for me to point my finger at."

"Ah! You took ownership!" he exclaimed.

"Why are you so excited?"

"It's the first step upon the path to Salvation!"

Salvation

None of them can by any means redeem his brother,
nor give to God a ransom for him: – Psalm 49:7

"Salvation? That's another thing that I don't get," I said with frustrated confusion.

"Get what?" Red asked sensing my mood.

"That whole salvation thing, what exactly are we supposed to be saved from?"

"I think you're asking the wrong question."

I retorted, "Well, what exactly should I be asking?"

"What's being salvaged?" he said without a moment of consideration to my question.

"Salvaged?" What does being salvaged have to do with being saved?"

"Most people associate salvage with something you do with boats and boat cargo."

"Exactly! What does it have to do with salvation?"

"They both have the same root that means *to save.*"

"Are you saying that experiencing salvation is being salvaged and being salvaged is being saved?"

"What I'm saying is that when you're seeking to figure out the meaning behind salvation, seek to understand a salvage operation."

"Salvage operations focus upon saving the vessel and the cargo."

"Exactly!" Red said with vigor.

"Are you saying the entire basis behind salvation is to rescue what you can?"

"That's a nice way of putting it. But in truth, it's usually rescuing *you* from *yourself*."

"I'm not clear on that. Please explain this further."

"Sure, typically people tend to blame outside sources and

other people when they experience the undesirable consequences of their choices and decisions.

"So? I see that all the time!"

"Yes," Red said with an intonation and a gesture that unmistakably indicated a deep-felt sadness. "I do too."

"And?"

"When they shift their focus off themselves as the cause of their dilemmas and discomforts and put it onto others, they never address the underlying cause and, as a result, they never accept that it is they who have to do the work to fix their situations."

"Are you saying their situations never receive the proper attention needed because they are always waiting for others to take upon themselves the responsibility for dealing with the consequences?"

"Yes."

"That's it?" I asked adding, "Is that all that you're going to say on it?"

"No, I have more."

"Well?"

"In the clearest of terms, they are waiting to be rescued from their irresponsibility and that waiting sabotages any efforts on their part to take responsible actions toward changing themselves and their situation."

"You mean they are waiting to be saved from their own irresponsibility?"

"Yes."

"From what I have seen, that's not likely going to happen."

"Indeed!"

"Are you saying that a true rescue operation is an inside-out job?"

"That's what I am implying," he said.

"So, that's what you mean by salvation is rescuing *you* from *yourself?*"

"Yes, but please tell me; how do *you* see that it's rescuing you from yourself?"

"From what I can tell, you're not going to see any difference in your situation until you first accept that you were the one who put yourself into it."

"Exactly!"

"And once you've accepted that, you accept too that it's your responsibility to make different choices and decisions than you did in the past to make enough significant changes so that you can redirect your life away from your present situation."

"Yes. It's only through these two specific actions that you have hope for salvaging the value you have left."

"So, the whole basis for salvation is to redeem yourself by investing in these actions?" I asked half-hoping I was spot on in my assessment direction.

"Isn't that the whole idea? You can't regain anything of value unless you invest in bringing it back into your possession...."

"...and you can't get your life back under control unless you accept that it was you that got it that way in the first place!" I added, putting on an apologetic face for interrupting him.

"I like that you're excited about this," he smiled.

"I am! Salvation was always put in front of me as if I had to accept that I couldn't do anything about it for myself and I had to have someone else do it for me."

"And?"

"I'm beginning to understand that I can do a lot to get the wheels rolling in new directions by simply accepting who I am and what I have done and take upon my shoulders the burden of changing how I both view my part in everything and how I'm the cause of much of my own distress."

"What about having someone else rescue you?"

"In these matters, that's simply not possible! To change things about myself, *I* have to *change me*," I said without hesitation. "I must be the one to do my transforming! No one can do this for me!"

"And?"

"That would also mean someone that is the new me would have to step in to salvage what was left of my old self."

"So, someone else truly *is* rescuing your old self?"

"Yes!" I exclaimed adding, "And that person is the new me!"

"You do realize that this dual mindset would mean that you will be of two minds during this process."

"How is it being of two minds?"

"You're going to have your old way of thinking and its momentum and habits. These will be at odds with your new way of thinking and doing. But that always occurs at the beginning of any valuable transformation."

"Darn!" I said instinctively. "That's going to be tough."

"Salvage operations are not for wimps, John," he said with a chuckle.

I laughed. It was making so much sense to me. It was also giving me a better understanding of the mechanics involved. So much of what I had heard in my youth was wishful thinking. The instructions I had received always made things worse because they inevitably led me to further detachment from the very cause of my situation – *me!* Everything I had been led to believe was counter to doing what I should have been doing all along, rescuing myself by stopping the very behavior that had driven me to not accept that I was the cause.

"Whatcha thinkin'?" he playfully asked, knowing full well that he was pulling me out of my thoughts and bringing me back to the conversation at hand.

"Just how simple it truly is when you lay it out on the table and look at it."

"How is it simple?

"One thing leads to another," I responded. "Every choice and decision that got me into whatever I was involved in and that I didn't like was part of a long chain."

"And?"

"That same chain of decisions and choices is as powerful at taking me out as it was at taking me in."

"They are indeed, John."

"So, the saving actually begins by taking ownership."

"Yes," he said. "And it continues when you recognize that you do have value worth investing in."

"Ah!" I said. "That goes back to the salvage of a ship and its cargo."

"Yes."

"If I recognize that I still have value, then I am worth investing in myself with better choices, better decisions, and better directions."

"Of course," he said adding, "No worthless ship or cargo is ever salvaged. It's only those that are valued that are worth the effort."

"So, another aspect of this is believing that you still have value regardless of the hole you've dug yourself into?"

"This is for certain. Why would you be motivated to save something that has no value whatsoever?"

"True," I said, pondering the question's ramifications. It was becoming clearer to me with every conversation and thought-filled aftermath that I had misunderstood so much in my life. Those misunderstandings had gotten into my way and caused a lot of wasted focuses along my path.

Securing the Gate

When I was a child, I spake as a child,
I understood as a child, I thought as a child:
but when I became a man, I put away
childish things. – 1 Corinthians 13:11

Red smiled at what I had just said and gave me a nod of knowing approval. "So, you do know firsthand what it's like to be an outcast by your own hand?"

"Yes!" I said emphatically. "I knew the moment I was outside too."

"How's that?"

"I felt as if life was *happening to me* rather than *for me.*"

"What changed your perspective?"

"I examined my choices and saw how they either contributed to or caused the situation."

"When you changed your perspective about your contribution to the situation, what occurred?"

"I felt empowered!"

"You felt empowered, even though you knew that you were in deep trouble?"

"Yes. I realized that if my choices caused my situation, then I could make new and different choices to change my situation to be more like what I really wanted."

"So, you weren't barred from re-entering the garden and simply walked right back in?"

"Wait!" I exclaimed. "Are you saying that what keeps people from walking back in is their thinking?"

"Actually, it's you that is saying this. I'm just trying to confirm what you already said."

"The ways Adam and Eve thought led them believe that they were outside the garden and it was this same way of thinking that kept them from reentering."

"Yes! But have you forgotten about those cherubim?" he responded looking at me like I had forgotten this tidbit of important information.

"You mean the ones holding the flame of a sword whirling in every direction?"

"Yes, them."

"I guess they would make for an intimidating reception."

"I agree."

"I imagine God put them there because He didn't want them to come back into the garden, at least, not then."

"As did Adam and Eve."

"Are you implying that God didn't put them there to prevent them from re-entering?" I asked.

"Remember how I said eating from the fruit from the tree influenced how they saw things?"

"Yes."

"And remember how they chose to see themselves as victims where everything that occurred was *happening to them* and not *for them, just like you did?"*

"Wait! Are you implying that they thought they were already outside the garden and viewed the cherubim as guarding the gate to prevent their re-entry?"

"I'm not," Red replied. "It's scripture that is implying this."

"So, they assumed by their perception of all the things that were occurring, that they were outside the garden. And they thought the cherubim were blocking their path."

"It certainly would be exactly how an irresponsible person would view things."

"This is something that I'm going to have to think about further."

"Good," Red responded as we turned a corner and I found, to my surprise, that we were right back at the entrance-way to the garden. My traveling companion smiled and asked, "How are you enjoying the garden's light so far?"

I looked at him, stunned. I realized exactly what he meant by his question. I had been receiving the garden's light all along, only I had been so focused upon reaching it that I hadn't realized I was immersed in it, until now. I was speechless.

"We don't often have such wonderful guests, John," Red said. "I hope you will come back some time and enjoy more of the light we have to offer."

Without any warning, the two garden's guards came over from the gated entrance and I soon found myself escorted outside with my head whirling with unanswered questions. What had just happened? Who were these people? Did I just experience something out of a dream?

It was then that I remembered the fruit that Sligh had tossed to me in the garden. Was it still in my pocket? I reached down and found it was still there. I pulled it out of my pocket and noticed immediately that there was a big bite already taken out of it.

"That's strange!" I thought as I scratched my head in wonder. *I don't remember it having a bite in it when I received it! "When did that happen?"* I heard myself saying out loud.

I had no answers to any of these questions. It was getting late in the day though and I was certainly tired from all the discourse within the garden. I started home. Remembering my promise to Bob, I chose to swing by his place first.

Part IV

The Reentry

Knocking at Heaven's Door

Metaphor

And the disciples came and said to Him, "Why do You speak to them in parables?" – Matthew 13:10

In an overwhelming haze, I found myself approaching Bob's place. He was already on his porch, swaying to and fro on his prized swing, ice tea in hand, and smiling. "Hello Fellow Traveler!" he shouted. "How was church?" he asked with a giggle in his voice.

I skipped right past my usual programmed formality. "It was closed for renovations, Bob," I said looking at him and inquired, "You knew that when you asked me, didn't you?"

"I'm not referring to the church that you first went to, John. I'm referring to the one within the garden; how was it?"

It was only then that I realized what he was really asking me. "Well, to be honest, it was quite an eye-opener."

"You're different today, John," he said in his typical straight-forward manner.

"I guess I am," I responded, not knowing how I was going to proceed in our exchange.

"So, how was your trip within the garden?"

"But how did you know that I went in?" is all that I could muster responding to his question.

"You're not quite as formal today. You appear to be in some deeply distracted thought."

"I'm swimming in light Bob and I don't have that firm footing that you said my journey would bring."

"Lots of light then?"

"Yes, but it all seems so unreal," I said with utter exhaustion in my delivery.

"What seems so unreal?" he asked in his usual *please tell me more* voice.

"The way all these books are written," I replied.

"Are we talking about the Bible?" he asked fully knowing to what I was alluding.

"Of course!" I exclaimed. "Adam and Eve, the serpent, trees... Am I supposed to believe all these things are real?"

"Real in what sense?" he asked forcing me to spell out the obvious.

"Real, as in, are they all historical characters?" I asked.

"Does it matter?" he said looking at me as if he had said something profound and was waiting for me to realize it.

"Of course, it matters!" I raised my voice to an almost uncomfortable volume even for myself.

"Why?"

"Because if it's not historical, then it's all just made up symbolism used to control the masses," I replied as if what I had said was truth itself.

"What if it is historical *within context?*" he asked hoping I would go in a more beneficial direction.

"Historical within context?" I asked reflexively. "What exactly does that mean?" I had no clue as to what he was saying.

"What if it is historic truth being conveyed through the context of allegory?"

"But I don't know what that means. Can you give me an example?"

"Sure. What if historically, the probability of someone using their right hand, rather than their left hand, dominated the majority of encounters between people?"

"And?"

"What if you wanted to communicate this historic probability by telling a story where the characters in the story used their right hand rather than their left hand?"

"Are you telling me that the writers of the biblical books were communicating historic human truths through parables and allegories?" I blurted.

"What I'm telling you is that the stories within the Bible's books are intended to communicate truths about being human. When you focus upon them as if they were actual singular historical events rather than historical truths conveyed through stories that occur all the time, you miss the entire point of what was written."

"But that's the point. Burning bushes, angel wrestling, and water turning into wine events don't occur all the time. Those things make these stories quite unbelievable."

"They can be if you take them to be factual instead of taking them as vehicles for communicating the truths that surround and express the human condition."

"How about giving me an example?" I requested.

"Sure. Take sacrifice for instance."

"Sacrifice?" I said, looking at Bob as if he had said something absurd.

"Yes, John. Sacrifice is the underlying theme of the whole garden experience."

I looked at him, blinking several times trying to drive his comment into a region of my brain that would help me get a grip on what he just said. I must have looked like a deer blinded by headlights to Bob who just waited patiently for me to make the necessary mental connections to further our conversation. It definitely *did not* come easily.

⌗————————————⌗

159

Sacrifice

Greater love has no one than this: to lay down one's life for one's friends. – John 15:13

"You appear to be in quite a state of confusion," Bob said as he broke into my silence.

"It's this sacrifice theme you just brought up."

"And?" he asked prodding me to expand on what was going on within my mind.

"Why does someone have to die?"

"What do you mean?"

"This whole sacrifice thing... why does there have to be a sacrifice and why does it require death?"

"It's the nature of getting things done."

I fired back, "Are you saying 'getting things done' requires death and sacrifice?"

"Yes," he said, not going any further with his response.

"You're going to make me pull teeth on this aren't you?" I said to him fully aware that this was going to require some effort from me to get a full answer.

"Of course, I am. All the best insights come out of an earnest personal investment. When you don't do what's necessary to bring these insights forth, they're never valued as much; this especially when you're just given the answers. Appreciating outcomes of hard work is incredibly important."

I sighed. I knew from experience that he was right. I could not remember a single time in my past when I have ever appreciated insights and information that were just handed to me. It was only that light which I had to struggle and bleed for that made me appreciate what I had received.

And it was at that moment that I realized why sacrifice needed blood! It was a metaphor for what must be offered to bring about something most desired.

"You have a way of triggering insights, my friend."

"How so?" he asked with a grin.

"There's a connection between obtaining goals and sacrifice."

"Yes, indeed!"

"To accomplish anything of significance, there are required decisions to be made."

"And what is the root of the word *decision*?" he asked playing along with my flow of thought.

"The whole word is built upon having to cut off options that will not get you what you need!"

"Options that will not support the outcome you truly want?"

"Yes, and if I truly want to bring about an outcome, I have to say goodbye to any activity that doesn't support it. That means I have to cut off and let die anything, activity or situation that is superfluous to my goal. This even includes relationships with some people!"

"Gotta sacrifice them?" he said facetiously with a smile.

"Absolutely!" I replied with vigor.

"How does this play into blood sacrifice?"

"It's a metaphor! It represents the investment of one's very being into making something occur. It's not actually spilling the blood of an animal or a human. It's about spilling your spiritual blood and how you're investing your very being in decisions and directions that support your commitments."

"Isn't that what passion is all about?"

"Passion?" is all that I could mutter at that moment, trying to grasp what Bob was conveying

"Passion is what we experience when we willingly embrace whatever suffering is necessary to get what we want."

"How does this play into sacrifice?"

"People truly filled with passion think nothing of making sacrifices. To them, suffering is just a part of the journey and it's sometimes a necessary means to desired ends, even if it means that they must suffer to get what they want."

"Can you provide me an example please?"

"Sure. What about the old you that you've mentioned?" he asked hoping I would make the connection by his new focus.

"The old me?" I said uncertain as to what he meant.

"Yes. We covered this before. What does the new you, the one who is committing himself to go in new directions, require of the old you? This question includes all the things that the old you might try to put in the way to continue in your familiar comfort zone. You know, to prevent the new you from succeeding with the changes that you now want to accomplish."

"You make it sound like the old and new me may not be in total alignment on the new goals."

"It happens a lot. Haven't you ever heard that *old habits die hard.*"

"Alright," I said with a sigh of resignation. "I get it. New directions require new habits and the elimination of old habits and ways of being that might get in the way and sabotage or hamper the new directions."

"Might?" he said with that same facetious playfulness I'd come to appreciate that drove points home in a gentle manner.

"Yes! Might and typically do. Okay, satisfied?"

"I'm not in this to be satisfied. I'm in it to assure that you're as clear as a bell in what you seek."

He was right of course. There wasn't a time I could remember that he had ever engaged me in any conversation where he didn't have my best interest in mind. I realized the connections. They were obvious.

"Is that what you mean when you told me that I would *'have to be totally willing to travel an unsettling path wrought with grief if I wanted more light?'*" I asked.

"What do *you* think?"

I remained silent in my thoughts and Bob didn't press me. I knew that sacrifice would almost be brimming with grief and upset. That's its very nature.

I finally spoke up, "Parts of the old me would have to die. To move beyond where I currently am, I would have to sacrifice those parts of me that would delay or prevent my future success."

"So, you're saying metaphorically, you'd have to sacrifice a part of you to achieve an outcome you had never achieved before?"

"Yes. It's clear to me that this is what the Old and New Testaments both refer to when sacrifice is called for."

"True, and I think there's more to it."

"What's that?" I asked curiously.

"When you get involved in a sacrificial situation, you're also making a covenant."

"A covenant? You mean like *an agreement?*"

"Absolutely! It's an agreement between your current and your future selves."

"Not with God?" I replied seeking clarity on this one point.

"How can God not be involved?" Bob asked rhetorically.

"But God doesn't have to be part of it," I said as if I was trying to convince myself.

"It's kind of impossible to exclude God."

"So, even if I hadn't thought about God being part of my deal with myself, it's impossible to not involve God?"

"Oh, for shame…" he sighed adding, "…all those double negatives…"

"But they serve a good purpose!" I quipped in protest.

"Let's clarify all of this. Are you making a deal with yourself?" he asked cutting to the quick.

"Well, yes."

"Isn't the spirit of God within you?"

"Ah!" I had made the connection.

"Go ahead and spell it out, John."

"By default, then, God animates all humans and by that condition, God is present and involved in all human activities." I sat in that insight for a moment and it felt quietly reassuring. "So, the moment I make a sacrifice, it's with the understanding that I'm making an agreement with my future self with God as my witness."

He smiled. He had seen me arrive at another level of understanding, but, not missing a beat, he then started to press me further. "And how does this relate to old and new Testament themes?" he asked, pushing me toward the very reason I started this discussion.

The Idol of Innocence

*Yeshua told his disciples, 'If anyone would come
after me, let him deny himself and take up his cross
and follow me – Matthew 16:24–28*

"I'm very uncomfortable with even the notion of sacrifice
though," I said in a bit of a protesting tone.

"How's that?" Bob asked.

"I don't believe in this sacrificing of innocents to cleanse
ourselves of sins," I said indignantly.

"I'm a bit confused as to what you're referring," he said
inviting me to explain.

"I don't like the premise that for a human being's sins to
be washed away, the blood of something innocent must be
spilled for that sinner. It's disagreeable to me."

"Ah!" he said with quiet assurance. "I get what you are
saying now. What part of it do you disagree with?"

"That part about harming any innocent soul for the
benefit of another."

"Where are you getting this?"

"In the Old Testament, there are numerous references to
people sacrificing and animal, usually from their livestock
that is considered pure and innocent as atonement for their
sins."

"And what about in the New Testament?" he asked
egging me on to disclose all of my preconceived notions.

"The New Testament is far worse in this respect."

"What do you mean?" he asked continuing to hold the door open to my ideas.

"I'm told that sacrificing innocent livestock is no longer acceptable. To be cleansed, one must spill the blood of one specific innocent and pure human."

"Yes," he said unexpectedly. "That is the message that most people hear."

I heard his response and didn't know what to make of it. It was almost as if he were indirectly saying that there was another message that could be heard. Not wanting to leave this message unknown to me if he was implying this, I asked, "You say that as if there's something else that makes more sense."

"Come on, John. When have you ever known me to imply that there was another way of looking at things?"

He smiled and looked at me with deadpan eyes hoping I would giggle at his invitation to explore the topic further.

"You do it all the time. Now, give it up. I want to hear more!"

"Okay. What is the most difficult thing for people to face who have spent their life up to that point in denial of their responsibility for their choices and actions?"

"Accepting accountability?" I asked hoping I would nail the answer on the first shot.

"No. That's just a continuation of their denying responsibility. It's something deeper than that."

"Then what is it?" I asked pressing him for something more.

Bob looked like he was taking a moment to find the right words. From his look, I didn't think that he got into these types of conversations too often. He took a deep breath and said to me, "Let me respond by asking you this. When a person denies his culpability or complicity in an event and the evidence implies that he is guilty, what is he actually saying?"

"He's claiming that he's innocent," I replied without thinking too deeply about it.

"And what has to die for him to let go of that claim?"

"The lie has to die," I answered and then added, "That false image of himself as innocent has to die."

"Right! So, does he not have to deliberately sacrifice that image of innocence, shedding its blood, for him to accept that he is guilty?" Bob asked rhetorically.

I put my hands up to my head and mimed a huge burst occurring out of both sides of my head as if I had my brain exploding from the sheer impact of his question. He giggled as he recognized immediately that I got what he was asking and the implications thereof.

"Is this whole issue *psychological?* " I asked trying to confirm my suspicion.

"Of course it is. How could it be anything else?"

"So, it's not about having someone else's innocent blood being shed or spilled for me?" I asked. I paused a second to state the obvious as Bob listened with a knowing grin on his face. "It's about me accepting that I'm *not* innocent, reconnecting myself to what I was guilty of and in doing so I sacrifice that image of me being innocent and I do so with no reservations?"

"It's always about the guilty parties coming to terms with their transgressions. That's why it's so important to have a paradigm that assists him or her toward that end. That's the whole reason for these metaphors, allegories, and such. It helps people realize the obvious. It helps them move past the denial and into reality. From the very beginning, it has been difficult for human beings to connect with how their choices bring about results – especially when those outcomes are not what they want to accept as something caused by their choices."

I sat there mulling over what Bob had said. It felt true to the point that it overwhelmed me with a flood of memories that all reflected times in my life when I had not wanted to accept how I had caused my life to turn out the ways it did. I found my cheeks wet with tears. I didn't know if they were caused by joy or relief. They felt peaceful though. Another piece of the puzzle had fallen into place and all the teachings that I had been taught throughout my life, from both the Good Book and from experiences, folded back upon each other and life made a lot more sense.

"I'm the cause. I'm the source," I said finally.

"So, *you* and the *source* are *one*?"

"Wow!"

Bob just sat there smiling. He realized that I had finally gotten it.

"It's not about shedding anyone else's blood," I said calmly. "It's about my willingness to shed my own blood, the blood of all that I thought that I was – innocent and pure – and reclaim my contributions to my life."

"It always is, John."

"Then it's truly not just about confessing. Anyone can easily put forth that effort and still harbor a self-image of innocence."

"Yes, *easily* is an apt word."

"But to confess and then deliberately sacrifice that false idol of innocence one has within, nurtured behind the scenes where even one's conscious soul has difficulty realizing this. That takes some effort."

"Yes. And once one does this with true deliberation, one crosses over into a place that is unlike any place most people experience."

"Where's that?"

"Paradise."

"Paradise?" I responded in confusion. "What does Paradise have to do with letting a false image of innocence die?"

"Think through the ramifications, John," he said, inviting me to go further down a rabbit hole of thought.

"Ah! A worthy challenge!"

"Indeed, one that many people are unable to achieve."

"Due to?"

"Never taking it on!"

"Why not?"

"It's fear, John."

"What's the danger?"

He looked at me for a long moment. I didn't know if he was searching for words or the right words. The moment of silence lasted painfully long. He didn't say a word. It wasn't until I realized that he was waiting for me to answer my own question that I saw him smile.

"Okay," I broke in. "I get it."

He giggled but didn't say a word.

"The danger is not only seeing the truth but accepting who we truly are."

"And?"

Sharing that one word was his way of inviting me to continue. It was most annoying at times, especially when it required me to think further than just the most obvious.

"And, it also means that we are admitting that we both cause the outcome by our choices and that we are more in control than we want to admit to ourselves."

"And that means?" he said inviting me to once again continue further down the path with him.

I bit at it saying, "Meaning that we admit we are responsible. We cause things to unfold. We are more in control than we want to acknowledge."

"So how does that get us out of this self-created hell?"

"This admittance," I said pausing to take a breath. "It releases us from the hell we believe we put ourselves in when we deny our culpability. By declaring our part, we open the doors to Paradise…"

"…when we choose to stay honest with ourselves about our personal contribution to our lives?"

"Exactly!" I exclaimed. "As long as we blame others for the hell we put ourselves in, we will never recognize that we *built* the place."

"And if we are that powerful?"

"Then we can build ourselves out of it, or at least start with accepting that it is a place we built not with our hands, but with our choices."

"Your words sound vaguely familiar," he said grinning from ear to ear.

I knew he was right, but there was something else on my mind that had me focused elsewhere. I spoke up trying to find the words, "There something more here."

"What's that?"

"To get into that Paradise state, you must be willing to do more than just sacrifice that false image of innocence."

Bob leaned in with anticipated delight. It was if he already knew what I was about to say, but held himself back as to make sure that I was uninterrupted. He looked at me waiting for me to say more.

"To get into Paradise, you must be willing to die!"

"Literally?"

"No," I responded as if to imply his question was silly.

But he knew what I meant to say and invited me to state the issue more clearly by asking, "Metaphorically?"

I looked at him and realized he wanted me to say more. "The false image dying is not enough. Who we are, the person who brought us into our hell, *must transform*. The spirit that had guided all the denial, that outran accountability and that acted irresponsibly, it had to die and be replaced with a character and spirit that no longer made or even desired to make these bad choices."

"So, one doesn't physically die, but one must transform in spirit to bring about paradise for one's self and do so in such a way that the previous thoughts and manners die?"

"Yes!" I said as if to say, "That's it!"

"So, sort of willingly going to the cross, right?"

I looked at him and didn't say a word. I knew exactly what he was implying. It was pretty clear that the way to Paradise included a willingness to be crucified, like it or not.

Just the thought alone was a tough cross to bear.

cx————————————80

The Cross-Examination

And Yeshua said unto him verily I say unto thee to day shalt thou be with me in paradise. – Luke 23:43

"Wait a minute!" I said to Bob. "Wasn't there a passage in Luke [32] about Paradise?"

"Yes. The passage in Luke was where Yeshua said to the robber nailed to the cross next to Him that the robber would be in Paradise with Him."

"I never understood that."

"Understood what?"

"Why did Yeshua tell the robber that he would be in Paradise with Him?"

"Why do you *think* Yeshua told him that?"

"I assumed that the robber accepted Yeshua as his Lord and Savior."

"How did you come to that conclusion?" he asked, hoping I would enlighten him as to the source.

"It's clear that the robber called him Lord."

"The word 'Lord' doesn't appear in every translation; especially from the original Greek. But where does it say that he accepted Yeshua as his personal Lord and Savior?" he pressed me for further clarity on the matter.

"Well," I said as I struggled to find the answer. "He didn't really. It's generally accepted that his calling Yeshua *Lord* was confirmation of that."

174

"It's assumed then?"

"I guess that's true," I said begrudgingly.

"So, if the robber didn't actually accept Yeshua as his personal Lord and Savior, then what did get him into Paradise?" he asked wanting me to show him the connection.

"I'd have to reexamine the text. I'm not clear on it."

"Have you examined what is written about the robber, John?"

"Yes. And it's not clear at all."

"I agree!" he exclaimed.

"Oh! It's not very clear to you either?"

"Yes. But there are some interesting twists in the story that I'd love to discuss with you."

"Great! What do you have in mind?"

"For starters, nowhere in the text does the robber directly accept Yeshua or say that he professed a belief in Him. But it does clearly say that Yeshua told him that he would be in Paradise with Him."

"Is there anything in scripture that indicates how the robber earned that right?" I asked with sincere interest.

"There's nothing that says it directly. However, there's at least one thing that the robber did do which, when you look back at the things we've talked about, indicates that he passed the G.O.E. Test."

"G.O.E. Test?" I asked looking at him reflecting that I had no clue as to what he was talking about.

"Yes. It's an acronym for the Garden of Eden Test."

"What's that?"

"It's the actual test that Adam and Eve were given in the garden."

"An actual test?" I said with bewilderment. "What are you talking about, Bob?"

"It's clear that God did give Adam and Eve a test in the garden and they failed it," he said matter-of-factly.

"Oh," I said making what I thought was a connection. "But what does that have to do with the robber on the cross? He broke at least one law and he got nailed for it. How did Adam and Eve's failing a test I the garden earn the robber passage into Paradise?"

"Those are some great questions and solid connections. It was what the robber did that Adam and Eve didn't do that got him safe passage."

"Neither Adam nor Eve accepted Yeshua as is required, but the robber must have!" I guessed.

"Did he?" he replied as if asking me to enlighten him as to something that he might have missed.

"The robber acknowledged Yeshua as *Lord* and asked Yeshua to remember him as He came into His kingdom."

"That's what some of the translations claim, John," he said. "But the word 'Lord' and the term 'His kingdom' do not appear in every translation," he continued. "If you want to split hairs, the robber also referred to Yeshua as 'this man' [33] when he was rebuking the other criminal for mocking Yeshua. Why do you think he referred to Yeshua this way?"

176

I didn't hear what he was asking of me. I was reeling with confusion. When I finally gathered myself together a little, I asked, "Are you saying the translations are wrong?" I fired this back at him as if he was calling my statement a lie.

"I really don't want to focus on these other tidbits that distract us from the important points. I'm trying to show something that the robber did which Adam and Eve did not do. Actually, to be more specific, the robber did two things that they didn't do."

"Well, what are the two things the robber did?" I asked sharply.

"Good question! Let's explore that." It was clear that he was glad to see that I was actually interested. "Do you remember the robber's first comment to the other criminal?"

"Yes. He rebuked him and said that the two of them deserved the punishment they were receiving. That was the first action that the robber did that was different from those taken by Adam and Eve."

"Agreed. What's the other thing that the robber did?"

"He said that Yeshua was innocent and that He did not deserve to be punished. That was the robber's second different action."

"Indeed! And in those two statements, he did two distinct things. Can you spell them out?"

"Yes. The first thing that he did was to state that he himself deserved his punishment."

"Meaning what?"

"That he was to blame for the situation he was in and that he was not blaming anyone else for the choices that had put him in his situation."

"Agreed," he said. "And his second action was?"

"His second action was to point out that Yeshua was innocent and didn't deserve what was occurring to Him."

"What does that mean?"

"It means that the robber indirectly stated that no innocent party should be made to suffer undeservedly, including Yeshua."

"So, the robber acknowledged the very two principles that Adam and Eve refused to admit prior to their being evicted from the garden," he summarized.

I looked at him like I was at a loss for words. He didn't know if I had understood the ramifications he had presented to me. I appeared to be overwhelmed by deep thoughts. Slowly he saw something stirring within me as I brought myself back to life and back into our conversation. "Are you saying that Yeshua told the robber that he would be in Paradise with Him just because he took ownership of his situation and acknowledged that no one who was innocent should have to suffer undeservedly?"

"Scripture is saying this. I'm merely reading it and connecting the dots. And that's what I suspect the writer of Luke did when he wrote his Gospel."

"Luke reported the conversation on the cross to stress what you just said?"

"But, Luke wrote down the conversation differently from how the writer of Mark did," [34] he responded and purposefully put off answering my question.

"What did Mark report?" I asked with a curious tone.

"He wrote that there were two criminals crucified with Yeshua and that those who were crucified with Him mocked him." [35]

"Wait a minute," I interrupted him, "that's in direct conflict with what Luke reported!" I appeared agitated by this as I looked at him to respond.

"Yes. And since Luke was written after Mark, it is clear that Luke wanted to communicate some further truth in the story by retelling what had occurred at the cross. In doing so, he added to the previous Gospel." Seeing the look upon my face he added, "And let's not get into whether Luke's addition to the story makes it a true contradiction or not. Let's focus upon the reason for what was communicated by Luke."

I thought about it for a moment. It was clear I was trying to rationalize what the Good Book revealed. "So that he could make people aware of the not so obvious connections between what the robber did do and what Adam and Eve didn't do in the garden?" I asked in disbelief.

"What's that?"

"He accepted accountability for his choices. Adam and Eve didn't."

"And?" he said, prompting me for more.

"And he willingly embraced the suffering he brought upon himself by his choices."

"Good! You're seeing the connection."

"With your help…" I added.

"All I did was point out the possible inconsistency and the likelihood that Luke wanted to communicate something vitally important for future generations to consider when they took the time to look for the connections. You did the rest."

"It's a lot to think about."

"I agree. Would you like a further connection to ponder?"

"Sure!"

"Yeshua had more to say about getting into Paradise," he said, winking at me and waiting for me to respond.

I thought about it for a moment and then smiled. Bob did too and he braced himself for my next question.

Paradise

> *He who has an ear, let him hear what the Spirit says*
> *to the churches. To him who overcomes, I will grant*
> *to eat of the tree of life which is in the Paradise of*
> *God.'... [Then] he showed me a pure river of [the]*
> *water of life, clear as crystal, [coming from] the*
> *throne of God and of the Lamb,... in the [middle of*
> *its street]. On either side of the river was... the tree*
> *of life, ... – Revelation 2:7; 22:1-2*

"Why Paradise Bob?" I said in protest. "It's not Heaven. They are two entirely different places."

"What are you saying?" Bob replied.

"Paradise is a garden separate and distinct from Heaven."

"Have you examined the scriptures closely?"

"I thought I had. Have I missed something?" I asked.

"It was obvious that the second robber was referring to the afterlife when he talked with Yeshua while they were being crucified."

"Do you mean when he asked Yeshua to remember him when He entered into His kingdom?" [36]

"Yes. It's a metaphor for the afterlife and it's clear that the robber believed in it because he would not have asked Yeshua to remember him after their deaths if he had meant something else," he said with confidence.

"But Yeshua changed it up and used the word *Paradise* in His response," I retorted in protest. "Yeshua wasn't really addressing the robber's request."

181

"Was Yeshua referring to the robber's request for Yeshua to remember him when Yeshua entered into His kingdom?"

"It makes sense that he was. However, why didn't He just say that He would remember him instead of telling him that they would be together in Paradise?"

"That's a great question! But was Yeshua avoiding the request or was He taking His response to the next level?"

"Admittedly, it's clear that He was not avoiding the request. It appeared that Yeshua was letting the robber know that they would be together in the afterlife."

"How did you arrive at this conclusion?" he queried.

"Yeshua went beyond saying that He was going to remember the robber. Yeshua went past that request and claimed that the robber was going to be with Him."

"Was Yeshua going to go to the Father?" Bob asked.

"Scripture tells us that was His intended destination. But it doesn't clearly say that Paradise and the intended destination were one and the same."

"The reference to Paradise is used three times in the New Testament," he added.

"Ok!" I exclaimed. "Does the context of any of the three tell us something about what Yeshua meant by using it?"

"Yes. But don't you think that information is moot?"

"Why would it be moot?"

"The robber was promised by Yeshua to be allowed to enter into Paradise with Him. That's the important point!"

"You mean *Eden*?" I asked more in a tone of requested confirmation.

"Yes. There are many translations out there that confirm this. But some translations claim that Paradise is Heaven or the presence of God. Regardless of how Paradise is defined or whatever source you might want to believe, it is clear that Yeshua was saying that the robber was destined to be there and, what's more, to be there with Yeshua."

"I can see how Eden and the presence of God would apply. However, how can we connect Paradise with Heaven?"

"That's a great question!" Bob exclaimed and then he held his hand up signaling that he needed a moment to think his response through. It was clear from his silence that Bob was building his reply. He then said "Please look at the other two New Testament references. Both refer to Paradise and, in one of them, it claims that the tree of life is there as well. Scripture says this is where God's throne is in place. Isn't the garden of Eden where the tree of life is supposed to be?"

As I should have expected, I was a bit overwhelmed by what we were discussing at this point. I saw many of the connections and what I saw made sense to me. I finally said, "So, the Kingdom of Heaven, the Kingdom of God, Paradise, the Garden... they're all part of the same complex?"

"John," he said to focus my attention. "Did Yeshua say that the robber would be in Paradise with him?"

"Well, yes," I said somewhat taken back since I thought I was on to something grand.

"We can easily get caught up in trying to figure out what Yeshua meant by His promise to the robber. Did He mean Heaven, God's kingdom, or Eden's garden? They're all distractions from the issue at hand. Yeshua said that they would be together in Paradise."

"But did He mean the garden in Eden, an earthly Paradise, or a celestial Paradise?"

"Why do you ask?"

"It was quite clear from scripture that they were both crucified. That's a death sentence. That would mean, since they would no longer have a living body, that Yeshua meant a celestial Paradise."

"So, you're back to, is Paradise referring to something other than the garden in Eden?"

"I guess I am. Didn't you say that there are two other mentions of Paradise in the New Testament?"

"Yes, I did."

"What was it that they said?"

"One says that the Apostle Paul was taken up into Paradise for a glimpse. Some interpretations say that it was Heaven. [37] The other reference to Paradise is where the tree of life exists where those who overcome are given permission to eat of it. Another scripture claims that this same tree was flanking a river that flowed from the throne of God." [38]

"So, it's pretty clear they're all within the same complex," I said as if to put it all to rest.

"If we were to take the scriptures at face value, the celestial Paradise would have the tree of life within this Paradise and the tree of live would be part of it."

"And that is where the robber was promised to be with Yeshua."

"That makes sense," he said with a wink. "Do you think there is a difference between Heaven and Paradise?"

"If you're in Paradise, does it truly matter? God's throne

is there. The tree of life is there. Even Yeshua and the robber are there."

"Yes!"

"But what about judgment?"

"What about it?"

"What if the robber made it to Paradise and then, after he was judged unworthy, he was kicked out?" I said still trying to make sense of it all.

"So, you're saying that Yeshua was keeping His word to the robber about being in Paradise together initially before God kicked him out for being unworthy?"

"Exactly?"

"But wouldn't that then put Yeshua in the same category that people put the serpent?"

"What category was that?"

"Telling half-truths!" he said, leaving me stunned with something that I had not considered.

"I don't want to believe that Yeshua would tell the robber a half-truth, and hide the ultimate destination from the robber to give him a hope that would be cruelly dashed."

"Then, you've made a choice."

"What choice is that?"

"You choose to have faith that Yeshua was telling the robber the whole truth when He told him that they would be together in Paradise and that was absolute and without any unspoken and undisclosed sidebars."

"Yes," I said without any hesitation. "I have indeed!"

The Burley Cherubim

> *... they four had the face of a man, and the face*
> *of a lion, on the right side: and they four had the*
> *face of an ox on the left side; they four also had*
> *the face of an eagle.* – Ezekiel 1:10

"I did notice an ongoing inside garden joke though," I said changing the direction of what was clearly an intense conversation.

Bob smiled and asked, "Just one?"

"This was one that stood out for me above any others."

"And?"

"The reference to the burley cherubim..."

Bob laughed. "Oh yeah!" he giggled. "That's definitely an inside joke!"

"I don't get it!"

"Would you like to get it, John?"

"Sure!"

"Look up!" he said as he got up out of his swing seat and stepped out from under his porch.

Not knowing what Bob was asking, I responded, "Like now?"

"Yes, now! Look up into the sky and tell me what you see."

It was a clear sky that was before me. The stars were out and I could actually make out the Milky Way. Bob's location was certainly made to order if you were a star gazer. I didn't really know to what Bob was referring, but I gave it my best shot. "Stars?" I asked.

"And what do stars form, especially in the minds of ancient men?"

"Constellations?"

"Yes. Exactly!"

"But what does this have to do with burly cherubim?"

"Have you ever looked at the description of cherubim?"

"Yes," I said with great affirmation. This one I did know! "Four faced four-winged fourfold creatures."

"And the faces are?"

"The face of a man, a lion, an ox and an eagle." I smiled like I had just gotten an "A plus" on a test.

"Yes. Now which constellations have those exact faces?"

"Aquarius, Leo, Taurus, and Aquila," I replied with a glowing smile. I don't think Bob knew that I had developed a passion for stargazing when I was younger and I knew this stuff like the back of my hand.

"Good!" is all that Bob said to my proud display of astronomical knowledge.

"Well?" I said, hoping there would be more to it.

"Well, what?"

187

"What's the connection?"

"Think about where these constellations are in the heavens," he said without any implied pressure to respond quickly.

I thought about it for a second or two and then I responded. "They're pretty much the four seasons."

"Meaning?"

I thought about it for a minute more, wanting to make sure I had it right. Leo becomes visible in the Northern Hemisphere around the spring equinox and is easily identifiable through May. Aquila is visible in the northern hemisphere's summer sky. Aquarius is visible in the fall. Taurus passes through the sky from November to March and is most visible in January; that's our winter-time. I spoke up finally, "Each face is found in one of the four seasons Bob," I replied.

"So, could you look up in the night sky at any point in time and tell from what you see where you were within the year in regards to the seasons?" Bob asked with a wink.

"Okay," I said conceding to the vague theme. "I guess so. But what does all this have to do with the burley cherubim inside joke?"

"We'll get there. Let's continue to focus on these constellations. If you have cherubim knowledge, you know exactly where you are in the seasons of life. This information was important to ancient people since each season brought different life conditions and challenges that had to be dealt with appropriately."

"And that included preparations for what was to come," I added, emphasizing the importance of seasonal awareness.

"Yes. Such knowledge meant life or death," Bob interjected. "They were crucial to humanity's existence."

"So, what's the basis behind the joke, Bob?"

"In scripture, why does it say the cherubim were placed in the Garden in Eden?"

"To guard the way of the tree of life," I said by rote.

"Exactly. That's what it says in the translation. But the key is *understanding* what that phrase means."

"Oh, that's simple," I said not waiting for his next question. "They're placed there to prevent reentry!"

"That's what a lot of people think."

"Are you implying there's another way to read this?"

"But of course. Think about the possibilities."

"Of reinterpreting the statement?" I asked with uncertainty.

"Yes," Bob said looking at me as if to expect more. "Think it through."

"Okay. I'm up for it. Where do we begin?"

"Start by examining your premise."

"That they are there to prevent reentry?"

"Precisely!"

"Are you implying they were not there for that job?"

Bob pulled out his flashlight and pocket Bible and flipped it open to Genesis 3:24. Darn, he sure did come prepared. He pointed down at the passage. "Read the line again and *think*. If the message was to communicate something other than preventing re-entry to the garden, what other message might it convey?"

I looked down at the line. I read through it several times and I could actually feel my facial expression change when I realized the not quite so obvious. I heard Bob giggle. He was looking at my new expression. As I examined the line it became clear that I had assumed they were put there to prevent re-entry. I had never considered that those cherubim might have been put there to make sure that the entrance remained open for those who wished to reenter. I looked at him and spoke. "Bob, this is *amazing*!"

"Ain't it though!" he snickered as if he had just pointed to a gem and I saw and grabbed it.

"All these years I had assumed those cherubim were put there to prevent re-entry, guarding the garden to keep people out."

"And now?"

"It's clear they were placed there as a beacon."

"Oh, I like your choice of words..."

I interrupted him. "I chose them precisely because of what I saw in the sky Bob." I stopped and searched for the right words to express the connection. "God put cherubim into the heavens to show us the way *of* the tree of life."

"Not '*to* the tree of life', but '*of*' it?" Bob interjected.

I looked again at the line within scripture. "Yes Bob, it's pretty clear once I saw to reject the notion that they were put there to prevent re-entry, it became clear that the real reason was to protect a way of life that has been long forgotten by modern humanity."

"Which is?"

I reviewed my experience in the garden. My entry had been blocked initially by the guards. But after I had told them a little about myself... and then it hit me! It was just after I had admitted that it was my own fault that I was there at the entrance to the garden that the one guard had said that I passed the test that I earned the right to enter the garden.

So it wasn't an inside joke. It was an unspoken acknowledgement!

Tilling the Soil

...and there was not a man to serve the soil.
– Genesis 2:5

Bob saw I was deep in thought and he broke into my silence. "So, I take it from your experience that you got your soil tilled," he said without any warning.

"Got my soil tilled?" I responded not knowing what the reverend was saying?

"The crew in the garden!" he replied asking "Did they till your soil?"

Not really understanding the question, I fired back, "Bob, please, back off on the metaphors. I'm still coming down off the trip."

"Fair enough," he said with an understanding tone. "Did your conversations with the crew in the garden overturn what you had once firmly thought that you knew and did your experience give you a lot more to think about?"

"Good Lord Yes!" I exclaimed. "They definitely did this all through our rich and thought-provoking exchanges."

"That's what I meant. The act of tilling the soil overturns earth that has been so compacted that nothing new can grow well within it, that is, if anything could even take root."

"Ah!" I said suddenly realizing the connection between the tilled soil and what occurred for me. "The scriptures
192

certainly do reveal how important tilling is. The soil must be tilled just right in order to properly receive the seeds of future crops."

"And you've gotten both the seeds and the tilling part [39] taken care of through your trip today, correct?"

I sat there in quiet contemplation of what Bob was asking. I unquestionably had been given a whole bunch of seeds and the soil of my past understanding was absolutely overturned and left receptive to them. "I'd have to say that did indeed occur, Bob."

"You're probably wondering what's next."

I looked at him and blinked, trying to drive into my mind what he had just stated. "What's next?!" I heard myself screaming inside my head. I had just gotten hit by a landslide of light and I was still being carried down an unsettled slope toward a destination that I knew I would never come back from. "What's next? Indeed!" I heard myself saying out loud without realizing it.

"I'd suggest you let the seeds settle in and germinate. You're newly tilled soil and you need to let yourself settle a bit before you start nurturing..."

"Newly tilled soil!" I shouted. I had just made the connection! I rattled a whole string of thoughts out loud to Bob. "I'm just like Adam! I'm made of earth just like him! Soil!!!"

"And?" Bob asked smiling and prodding me to continue.

"And our job as animated humus is to till our soil!"

"What does that mean?"

"It means we cannot as soil-based creatures allow the soil we are made of to get so deeply settled and compacted that nothing new can grow in it."

"So, you have to do what?"

"We have to continually *till* ourselves!" I exclaimed. "Literally, humanity was put into the garden to till ourselves so that we would be receptive to seeds."

"Sort of like, being ground that has the ability and the willingness to maintain its own fertility?"

"Yes!" I said in excitement. "We can never let ourselves get to the point where we become so rock solid that we kill our own growth potential. Tilling *keeps* us alive! It also keeps us viable to grow things within us."

"Is that what you think it meant when God said there was no one to till His garden?"

"You mean, the soil within the garden would, by its very nature, get to the point where it would become compacted over time and therefore stagnant?"

"Yes. It would need continuous tilling to remain fertile."

"And God put a tiller in His garden to assure that this would occur, forever!"

"What does that mean?"

"Humanity was put forth to assure that God's garden soil was kept viable and receptive to His seeds."

"Oh, now you're just sounding preachy," Bob said with a loud laugh.

"Hey now! The metaphor stands solid for this story. Humanity was put forth to assure God's garden was taken care of and didn't fall into disrepair."

"Disrepair?"

"Yes! The metaphor's pretty clear here. Adam was made of adamah, as was all of humanity."

"Adamah?" Bob asked prodding me to continue sharing.

"Adamah!" I said, not realizing that Bob was testing me. "You know, red clay…" And when I said this, my flow of words stopped.

"*Red* clay you say?" Bob asked with a little too much pleasure behind his tone.

"Wait! Could that be a nickname for Adam?"

"It sure does fit," he said with both a wink and a grin.

I sat there silent again. I just realized Red had been pulling my leg from the moment I met him. He had adopted a nickname for the very first garden tiller in recorded history and it had not become evident to me until now.

"Pretty cool play on words there, eh?" he smiled.

I smiled back and said, "I'll say it is!"

It had been a long day and I felt myself slipping into autopilot. "Bob, I think I'm way past saturation."

"Exhausted?"

"For sure! And I have a lot to process. Stopping by here has certainly helped though. Thank you!"

"You're most welcome," he said with a sincere tone.

"And thank you for asking me to attend church today," I said winking at him to drive home the point that I knew what he had done for me.

We soon said our good nights and I was shortly on my way back home.

Home Again

And they were both naked, the man and his wife,
and were not ashamed. – Genesis 2:25

"You okay?" Candy asked as I walked through our front door.

"Yeah," I said in a tired tone.

"You looked drained," she replied, looking into my eyes with concern.

"It's been a long but enlightening day," I let out a deep sigh. "I'm exhausted."

"Church was good for you then?"

"I didn't get to attend. At least, not the one I thought I was going to…"

"What?"

"Yeah… I forgot that the church was closed for renovations."

"Oh?" she said trailing off.

"It's my fault for not remembering to check."

"So, how did you spend your day?"

"I spent most of the day walking in the garden across the street from the church."

"The whole day?"

"Most of it," I said. "I dropped by Reverend Bob's afterward. The garden wasn't in my plans. But it turns out that it was for the best."

"You'll have to tell me about it tomorrow, John," she said. Candy knew when I was over-spent. She grabbed my arm and pulled me toward the couch and some quiet time. She always knew what was best for me.

Ouroboros

Now the serpent was the most cunning of any beast
of the field which the LORD God had made…
– Genesis 3:1

It was about a year later when a most unusual conversation occurred at work. I was in my office but I was once again thinking about the conversations I had within the garden when my associate, Veles, popped his head through the doorway.

"What are you so focused on?" he asked with a playfully stern tone. He was forever engaging me in the oddest conversations and this was another one of many that I knew was about to occur.

"I was just thinking over a memory I had from about a year ago. I'm still wondering how I could explain what I learned."

"What's the topic?"

"Original Sin, Veles. I don't think it's what people say it is."

"Well, no matter what people say it is, it's something I don't have to worry about," Veles said as if it were the God's honest truth.

"Worry about what?" I asked, not having a clue as to what he was referring.

"Paying for my sins," he said with the utmost confidence.

"What sins?" I asked, trying to figure out the connection he was making between the original sin that I have come to know and paying for sins in general.

"Any sin!" he retorted.

"Any sin?" I asked earnestly trying to pry some background information from him.

"Yes, John! Any sin!"

"What does that *mean,* Veles?"

"It means I have a clean slate," he replied and added, "I have a 'get out of jail free' card."

"How did you get that?"

"I accepted Yeshua's gift," he said without hesitation.

"Yeshua's gift?" I asked trying to get Veles to let me in on his great deal.

"Yes, John," he said with a tone of superiority as if to imply that I should know what he was talking about. "Yeshua's gift," he repeated.

"Forgive me for not getting it, Veles. What exactly are you talking about?"

"Let me spell it out for you, John. I do not have to pay for any of my sins. They have all been paid for and forgiven."

"How did this payment and forgiveness come about, Veles?"

"Yeshua paid the price for them. As a result, I do not have to."

"And I am asking you *how* He did this?"

"By suffering and dying for me," he replied and added, "and for suffering and dying for us all!"

"But how does His suffering and dying actually *pay* for your sins, Veles?" I pressed him.

"Don't you see, John? God demands a perfect sacrifice in order for sins to be forgiven," he said ignoring my question.

"Perfect? Do you mean a mature sacrifice or a flawless one?" I said hoping to prompt him to continue his unstated train of thought.

"Flawless, of course. And Yeshua is the perfect sacrifice!"

"Where exactly did you get this required flawlessness, Veles?" I asked half hoping he would actually have a decent foundation of thought behind his claim.

"It's right there in the scriptures, John," he spurted out. "Haven't you read them before?" he said as he made an effort to shame me into accepting his words.

"Yes, Veles. I have indeed read it and there are dozens of statements in the scriptures about being forgiven that don't require a flawless sacrifice."

Veles became uneasy in his manner. He didn't know what I was about to share but he looked like he was bracing himself for it. He looked at me sternly, as if to imply that I was foolish for even bringing to the table something that didn't require a perfect sacrifice and asked, "Like what?"

"I believe it clearly states: Forgive, and you will be forgiven," I reported.

"Well, yes, but…" he replied and I interrupted him.

"It also says: For if you forgive other people when they sin against you, your heavenly Father will also forgive you," [40] I added. "Where exactly is this flawless sacrifice requirement of which you speak?"

"Yeshua is the perfect sacrifice John," Veles repeated his words as if repetition alone would support his claim.

"And He suffered and died for you?"

"For me and for everyone else who accepts His gift."

"And you're totally okay with another human being suffering and dying for what you have done?" I asked trying to see if he understood the moral and ethical implications of his choice.

"Of course, I am, John," Veles said with a firm unwavering tone. "That's the whole point!"

"And you don't see anything wrong with that?"

He once again ignored what I asked him. "You don't get it. It's a God-given gift! You're making it sound sordid."

"But you're willingly embracing a arrangement where another soul suffers and dies for what you have done Veles," I repeated, hoping against hope that he would make the connection between his choices to do wrong and his conscious choice to allow another soul to suffer and even die because of his choices.

"Until you accept His gift and the freedom it affords you, John, you just won't understand," he said dismissively.

"Oh, I totally understand, Veles," I responded with a cautious delivery. "I understand you've made a conscious choice to try to outrun your accountability."

"How could that be, John?" Veles fired back. "I have been forgiven. My sins have been paid for. How could I be outrunning my accountability?"

"Have you made direct amends to those whom you have sinned against?"

"Well, no," Veles said. "But I don't have to, since all of my past actions have been forgiven and paid for."

"Do the people you sinned against agree with this? Has the suffering that you caused them been relieved? Have..."

"You're making this far too complicated, John," Veles interrupted with what came across to me as a resentful tone. "The gift is quite simple: Immortality in Heaven! And all you have to do is accept Yeshua's gift."

If Veles was anything else, it would be overshadowed by his dogmatic approach to things.

"Thanks, Veles!" is all I could muster in the face of his sheer single-mindedness. I knew from his responses that there was no direct way to ride this conversation out to a smooth finish. So, I decided to take a side road. "I see that you have faith that you have found something that works so well for you."

He exclaimed emphatically, "Yes! I have indeed!"

I decided at the moment to get up out of my seat and head for the rest-room. Perhaps some cold water on my face would help me bring back my focus.

I excused myself and, in a short moment, I was past Veles, out the door and on my way to refreshment.

 ☙————————————❧

The Pearly Gates

*Love does no wrong to one's neighbor [it never hurts
anybody]. Therefore love meets all the requirements
and is the fulfilling of the Law.*
– Romans 13:10 (Amplified Bible, Classic Edition)

I had gotten off early from work that day so I headed
toward the garden and the *Garden Club Café* to grab a bite
to eat and to work on some ideas for something I was
writing. When I got there, I found the usual crowd engaged
in conversation and enjoying the menu items.

I sat down in a nicely shaded spot, pulled out my laptop,
and fired it up.

Dawn was working this day and she came over to ask me
what fruit I wanted to partake of today. This was typical of
her. She tried to play up the theme of the restaurant's name
to have some fun with the patrons.

Without waiting for her to ask, I said, "I'll have a glass of
water with no ice please." It was part of our well-established
routine.

"With a bowl of sliced garden lemons on the side?" she
winked and smiled, already knowing full well my preferences.

"But of course!" I chuckled as she turned and headed
back toward the counter area door.

"Hey, John!" someone said to me as I turned around
toward the voice. It was my long-time buddy Jeff.

"Been here a while?"

"Not too long. It's good to see you."

"Same here. Are you waiting for anyone?"

"Not really. Care to join me?"

"I was hoping you'd ask," he said with a playful tone. Looking at my laptop, he asked, "What are you working on?"

"An interesting dilemma my friend," I said hoping to rope him into a good discussion.

"Ah! A worthy challenge!" he said with glee. "Count me in on discussing a solution!"

"But you haven't even heard what it is."

"I know enough about you that it's got to be a *good* one," he chuckled. "I wouldn't miss it for the world."

"Have you two decided what you're going to have," Dawn interrupted us as she approached.

Jeff didn't even look at the menu. He knew what he wanted and just smiled at her like he typically did. She looked at his smile, grinned at him, and said, "The usual, I take it?"

"But of course," he half-laughed adding, *"I know a good thing."*

"And you?" she turned to me and waited for my response.

"The same," I smiled.

"Great," she replied. "I'll be back real soon."

"That's interesting that you would word your response to me that way," I hinted at the coincidence of his last words having something to do with the dilemma I was working on.

"Stop teasing and let me in on it, John," he playfully demanded.

"Okay," I said smiling. "Are you familiar with Saint Peter's role at the pearly gates?"

"You mean the folk lore that places him as Heaven's gate keeper?"

"Yes. I know it's loosely based upon scripture but I want to use the scenario to stress a point."

"Awesome! I *love* stressing points! Fire away!" he said with enthusiasm.

"Thanks. What if the guy, whoever he is that's at the entrance to Heaven, is presenting a final test prior to anybody's entry?"

"Like a quality control last measure type of thing where he's inspecting the quality of the soul just before the point of no return?"

"Yes!" I chirped. "Exactly that!"

"Like what could he possibly ask a departed soul to determine if it deserves entrance into Heaven?" he asked with great curiosity.

"Yes."

"What do you have in mind?"

"I'm leaning toward something from the garden in Eden," I said hoping Jeff would pick up on the connection.

"That would be a nice twist," he said thoughtfully and added, "How about that issue we've discussed a few times regarding people taking or not taking responsibility?"

"Yes, but I want to go a step beyond that."

"Right, like taking ownership?"

"More along toward the accountability end."

206

"How about asking the soul if it was willing to be held to account for the choices it made over its lifetime?"

"Yes. There's that. But I want to take it even further than that."

"John," he said with a half-bewildered tone, "what could be further than that?"

"How about the suffering one has caused?"

"The suffering?" he sounded even more confused.

"Yes," I said adding, "In the story of Adam and Eve, it is implied that they were willing to allow others to suffer for their choices. That was a shortcoming that was the catalyst for their being thrown out of the garden."

"Ah!" he interrupted me. "And what you're trying to do is associate the entering into Heaven with the expelling of Adam and Eve from the Garden."

"Exactly!" I said with excitement. "Before their eviction, Adam and Eve were thought to be in Paradise. And Heaven is thought to be an afterlife Paradise."

"And what you are implying is that no one should be allowed into Paradise who cannot pass the test!"

"Yes. The G.O.E. Test!" I responded with a giggle.

"G.O.E. Test John?"

"Garden of…" I said to hint.

"…Eden!" he broke out laughing with delight. "Oh, that's a good one!"

We chuckled as we both took a sip of our drinks. "That's exactly what I am going for, Jeff. If the rules applied in the beginning, why would they *not* apply at the end and at a new beginning?"

"You're going to upset a lot of folks with that revelation, John," he said with a tongue-in-cheek grin.

"Yes, but only when they flunk the G.O.E. Test!" I fired back with a grin. "And they'll flunk the test the moment they blame me for their choice to be upset!"

Jeff giggled at my comment and asked, "So, what's the scenario going to be like?"

"I imagine Saint Pete asking the waiting soul, 'Are you willing to let another soul suffer to pay for your life choices.'"

"Isn't that a backwards way of addressing the – *if I had done something during my life that had caused others to suffer, would I be willing to take that suffering away from them if I could, even to the point of choosing to suffer myself so I could prevent anyone else from suffering for what I had done* – question?"

"Yes. The question would indirectly address the soul's conscious commitment to make any proper and deliberate amends for the suffering that it had caused to others. This means removing to the best of its ability the suffering it had caused up to actually taking that suffering upon itself if it could, so that other souls didn't have to."

"So, you want to go beyond the usual, 'I'm a sinner' repenting verbiage and you want to focus upon addressing the outcomes and impact of the sins," he summarized.

"Yes," I said adding, "The question would indirectly address the consequences of one's choices which, by default, would impact others, intentionally or not. And especially any undue suffering those choices created or will create."

"So, what if Saint Peter hears from the soul that it's willing to repent, but it wants another soul to suffer instead of accepting onto itself the suffering it had caused?"

"That's where I was going with this. Adam and Eve believed that they had been cast out of the garden because they didn't want to accept any consequences for the choices they each had made. Couple this with the ramification that by shifting the blame away from themselves, they were indirectly saying they wanted someone else to suffer, in their place, the outcomes of their choices."

"Okay," he said without hesitation. "The soul that willingly embraces allowing the suffering of others due to its choice is, by default, reenacting the irresponsible behavior that Adam and Eve exhibited when they were in the garden."

"And if they behave irresponsibly, why would God accept them into Heaven?"

"Based solely on your reasoning, God wouldn't," he replied hoping I would catch his play on words.

I groaned and smiled. "Good one!" I said adding, "But what if the entire guardian at the gate scenario is really just a ploy?"

"A ploy? A ruse implemented by a trickster?"

"Like Satan himself,"

"Wait a minute. Are you saying that the whole scene is to give this devil one more chance to capture a soul for Hell?"

"Why not? It's the best opportunity he can ever get."

"What do you mean?" he queried.

"Think about it. After a lifetime of struggles, believing that you are doing all the right things, and toeing the line that is put forth to you by your life-guides, you come to the gate thinking that you have arrived and all you have to do is answer a simple question and then you enter."

"I imagine a soul might be caught off guard by a seemingly simple question."

"Indeed! It would be the final test after a lifetime of tests, and you're right at the entrance to Heaven. What could possibly go wrong?"

"Well, you could say that you're willing to let someone else suffer for what you have done in life."

"And in that instance, this devil would have you based upon the protocols established in the beginning. God wouldn't even have to blow the whistle and tell you to get out of His pool. You wouldn't even get in."

We both cringed at the scene we had imagined. Satan wouldn't be a bad guy here. He'd be just enforcing God's edict established over six thousand years before.

"But what if it wasn't Saint Peter or Satan?" Dawn asked as she approached us once again, this time with our order.

"You mean it might be someone else putting the test question forth?" I asked.

"Yes," Dawn affirmed and added, "What if it was someone like a masked Yeshua asking the question?"

"Yeshua in disguise?" Jeff asked.

"Yes," Dawn replied. "Disguised so that the soul seeking entry wouldn't know Who it was dealing with."

"That would be quite a switch up indeed," I said.

"And there would be certain strength behind it, don't you think?" Jeff asked hoping I would take the statement and run with it.

"Especially for any soul who has accepted Him as its scapegoat to avoid suffering," I added.

"Can you imagine a soul's confusion being offered release from its suffering only to find that to accept such a release offer would be the antithesis of Christ-like behavior?" Dawn asked as she headed off to another table.

"It would go against everything that some souls were taught," Jeff said.

I agreed adding, "To be Christ-like in this instance, a soul would have to not let another suffer for anything the soul had done. To allow others to suffer because of its choices would have to be an unacceptable choice; the very choice that got Adam and Eve kicked out of the garden."

"So they would have to be Christ-like?"

"Yes, Christ-like. What do you think being Christ-like would be like?" I asked.

"Be like what?" he replied in his usual "you better explain yourself before I commit to another conversation direction with you" response.

"To be Christ-like in this respect."

"What respect?"Jeff asked with a bit of confusion.

"In respect to answering the very question our gate guardian posed to a soul asking to enter Heaven or Paradise."

"Oh! The one about a soul's willingness to have others suffer and die for things that it had done?"

"Yes," I said hoping Jeff would go further. I quickly prompted him with, "What are your best thoughts on this?"

"I imagine that if you asked most followers of what is said to be His teachings, they would tell you a litany of attributes that have to do with loving God and loving your neighbor."

"I agree. But what is being Christ-like when it comes to what Adam and Eve didn't do?"

"Do you mean, what did they lack that got them kicked from the Garden that Yeshua exhibited?"

"Yes! How does it all fit together in that respect?"

"For example?" he asked looking for me to give him a good one.

"Yeshua said that He and the robber were going to be in Paradise together."

"Okay?"

"What quality did Yeshua and the robber have that Adam and Eve didn't?"

"You mean, to be in Paradise together rather than being kept from Paradise like Adam and Eve were?"

"Exactly!"

"I suspect it has something to do with those two great commandments that He shared."[41]

"Loving God and neighbors?" I asked.

"Yes! That's what I'm thinking. And I think that applied to the question at the gate."

"Let me try to connect the two."

"Okay."

"I believe the question tests a soul's love of God and of fellow souls."

"Would you personalize it for me, John," Jeff requested.

"Sure. If you truly do love as Christ desired us to, then you would never allow another soul to suffer or die for what you have done or not done. *This would especially include someone else who has offered to suffer for you.*"

"So, based upon this, the only way past this gate question would be what?" he pressed the thought forward.

"It would be for you to turn the gate offer down saying that no one should ever have to suffer because of you, ever. I'll add to this, and no innocent person should be made to suffer for anything that they are innocent of."

"I like that! Truly personal," Jeff said with a tone of thoughtful compassion.

"And that explains why the robber went to Paradise with Yeshua."

"He said that Yeshua didn't deserve what He was going through…"

"…meaning no innocent souls should be made to suffer needlessly…"

"…and the robber owned his responsibility for his actions, too."

"He said that he deserved what he was going through."

"Exactly! Can you imagine the look on Yeshua's face when the soul He questions at this imaginary gate scenario you've created says that it would not want to have another soul suffer for the choices it made?" Jeff asked.

"I imagine it would be a mixture of relief and delight."

"Indeed. Especially since according to what is being peddled by many ministers, He was the soul that would likely have to suffer had that soul accepted the offer."

"But delighted too," I echoed adding, "He finally encountered a soul that made Christ-like choices also!"

"Had Adam and Eve done this, they would both still be in the garden enjoying all that fruit," he said jokingly.

"And we'd be having an entirely different conversation."

"Maybe we would, or perhaps we never left the garden and the entire tale was put forth to get us to realize it."

Our conversation got interrupted by my quick look at my watch. It was far later than I had thought it was and I knew I had to press forward to return home. I thanked Jeff for the great impromptu conversation and departed soon after gathering up my stuff. The conversation left me with a lot to digest.

Inspired by God

"Thus says the Lord, the God of Israel, 'Write all the
words which I have spoken to you in a book.
— Jeremiah 30:2

When I returned home, I was greeted by my lovely bride with our youngling still in her arms. The evening quickly turned to night and we were off to bed.

But I soon found that sleep was not on my body's schedule. I was restless. I could not get the events of the day and, more specifically, of the garden, out of my head. I also knew from experience that writing things out helped me both clarify my thoughts and helped me put things to rest. It was two-fifteen in the morning and my mind said it had had enough disturbed sleep. It was screaming at me, "Get out of bed and start typing!"

One thing was for sure. If I was going to get any sleep at all, I had better put down into writing what was disquieting my soul. This garden story was permeating every aspect of my life; my work, my leisure, *and even my dream states!*

It was at that moment that Candy rolled over and nudged me. I should have expected it. She had told me many times that she could hear me thinking while I slept. "Are you going to go down now or are you going to stew till day break?" she asked.

"It's that obvious?" I said almost with a scowl.

"Would I be talking with you this early?"

"Good point!" I replied.

I heard Candy giggle as she rolled over. She would be back to sleep in no time. As for me, sleep would not take me soon.

"So, this is what it means to be inspired by God?" I heard myself moan as I got out of bed and headed toward my downstairs office.

Candy snickered and muttered, "Own it, John.'

"Arrhhgg!" I grumbled lovingly as I descended the staircase and headed to the kitchen to brew a cup of hot tea. I thought, "There's no good reason I shouldn't have some caffeine coursing through my veins as I type out *the inspired words of God.*" I heard myself giggle as I realized what I was thinking. "Inspired words of God, as if!" I muttered.

As I prepared my tea, I found myself humming the opening baseline to the tune, *Stand By Me.* Its warm chords resonated with every thought that kept me awake.

I was soon in my office; eager to get underway. Before long, I had fired up my trusty word processer, took a deep breath, and typed in…

"Chapter I. The Good News

"It's showing a plus sign," she said, not quite knowing what it meant. "*…

Afterword

The Story's Origins

It was several years after my first early morning talk with Candy (mentioned near the beginning of this book) when I began teaching a few classes at a local school. It was then that I became aware of a pattern to my instruction.

I noticed that I was continually focusing some segment of one class on "personal discipline." Many of the students attending this class struggled with a lack of discipline in their lives. I dedicated ample time toward conveying to them methods that could help them to enhance constructive discipline for their benefit. As with many commitments of this kind, it also meant that learning material was required to bring this about.

Wishing to keep things simple, I went back to some of the many books I had sequestered on my shelf. I remembered reading years before about discipline in the first chapter (by that name) in M. Scott Peck's book "The Road Less Traveled."

I found that this was a great starting point for my students. A few years earlier, I had committed to memory the four tools Peck had recommended to bring about better discipline in life. I found that I was quoting these four tools continuously during these classes.

Knowing that it was much easier for people to remember stories, I had put myself to task to create some stories of my own. I began weaving short stories about each tool to "drive home" the importance of each of these disciplines and to make it easier for the students to recall each of these tools after they completed my class.

I soon noticed something wonderful happening. One specific story in my collection of stories began to take on a life of its own. It had to do with the discipline tool I most often referred to as "ownership." It had every element of taking on mature responsibility for one's life. Most of the students hearing the tale for the first time have come back to me and have shared the wondrous impact the story has had on their lives.

After telling the tale several times, I eventually dubbed it **"G3 Revisited,"** in honor of the third chapter of Genesis being the dominant contributor to this memorable Tale. Most students who heard this story immediately recognized this material as coming from the second and third chapters of the first book of both the Jewish and Christian Holy Scriptures. *G3 Revisited* was quite a powerful story with many unexpected twists and turns. Many of those twists and turns were woven into the story through a natural progression of insights shared by my students and gleaned by me as we collectively uncovered more information on the topic at hand.

Because of this ongoing process, I was left with two very powerful questions that brought about the most interesting conversations a coach, teacher, and facilitator could ever hope to engage his students in.

1) How do we today re-enact the sin in the garden in our everyday life?
2) How do we stop this process of re-enacting the sin so we can regain a paradise on earth?

What follows is the short story I created and shared with my students years ago about taking ownership of your choice, and the questions that followed.

☙————❧

G3 Revisited

In the Beginning, our main Character, *God*, got creative. He created all of creation and, since he was lonely and wanted to share His creation, included some companions in His effort; let's call them, *Adam and Eve*.

He put His companions into a wondrous garden and let them have free-rein. His only warning to them was to not eat the fruit of one specific tree because He knew it would change their lives forever.

God, feeling very accomplished by His great feats, went away for a little while and left His garden to be tended to by His companions.

Upon coming back, God realized all too soon that the two had eaten of the tree He had warned them about.

God first asked Adam what he had done. Adam immediately pointed his finger at Eve, implied that she tempted him and then at God for putting Eve there to tempt him.

God then asked Eve what she had done. Eve, seeing what Adam had just done, immediately pointed her finger at the serpent for deceiving her and, by doing so, implied that God had put the serpent there to deceive her into making her choice.

God immediately realized the game that was playing out before Him. His companions were not only making their own choices, but they were using their choices to try to outrun any accountability for their choices and they were blaming Him and others for what they had chosen to do.

He knew that these two would eventually eat from the other tree, the tree of life, and therefore live forever in his garden. As things were playing out, they would never learn to take any responsibility for the choices they were making.

He also knew what these choices would eventually do to His beautiful garden, day in and day out. They would make a mess of things fairly quickly and with no end in sight.

God would have none of this.

So, God blew His whistle and said, "Everyone! Out of My pool!" and He summarily placed these two irresponsible fools outside of His garden to experience their lives as the victims they chose to be and in hopes that their experiences would help them learn (sooner or later) to make better choices for themselves.

That is, until they realized their shortcoming, took ownership, and changed their irresponsible ways forever.

What do you think would have happened if Adam and Eve had each taken responsibility for their choices and had simply said, "Yes, I chose to eat," and left it at that? Do you think God would have responded differently if they had simply owned their choices without blaming others? Do you think He might have delightfully said, "Good! Let me show you another tree that might interest you?"

For what choices you have made have you tried to outrun your accountability and who have you blamed for your life choices? How could your life be different if you took blameless ownership of every choice that you have made and for all those that you will make into your future? How could doing this change your world for the better?

Genesis 2 - King James Version

[1] Thus the heavens and the earth were finished, and all the host of them.

[2] And on the seventh day God ended his work which he had made; and he rested on the seventh day from all his work which he had made.

[3] And God blessed the seventh day, and sanctified it: because that in it he had rested from all his work which God created and made.

[4] These are the generations of the heavens and of the earth when they were created, in the day that the LORD God made the earth and the heavens,

[5] And every plant of the field before it was in the earth, and every herb of the field before it grew: for the LORD God had not caused it to rain upon the earth, and there was not a man to till the ground.

[6] But there went up a mist from the earth, and watered the whole face of the ground.

[7] And the LORD God formed man of the dust of the ground, and breathed into his nostrils the breath of life; and man became a living soul.

[8] And the LORD God planted a garden eastward in Eden; and there he put the man whom he had formed.

⁹ And out of the ground made the LORD God to grow every tree that is pleasant to the sight, and good for food; the tree of life also in the midst of the garden, and the tree of knowledge of good and evil.

¹⁰ And a river went out of Eden to water the garden; and from thence it was parted, and became into four heads.

¹¹ The name of the first is Pison: that is it which compasseth the whole land of Havilah, where there is gold;

¹² And the gold of that land is good: there is bdellium and the onyx stone.

¹³ And the name of the second river is Gihon: the same is it that compasseth the whole land of Ethiopia.

¹⁴ And the name of the third river is Hiddekel: that is it which goeth toward the east of Assyria. And the fourth river is the Euphrates.

¹⁵ And the LORD God took the man, and put him into the garden of Eden to dress it and to keep it.

¹⁶ And the LORD God commanded the man, saying, Of every tree of the garden thou mayest freely eat:

¹⁷ But of the tree of the knowledge of good and evil, thou shalt not eat of it: for in the day that thou eatest thereof thou shalt surely die.

¹⁸ And the LORD God said, It is not good that the man should be alone; I will make him an help meet for him.

¹⁹ And out of the ground the LORD God formed every beast of the field, and every fowl of the air; and brought them unto Adam to see what he would call them: and whatsoever Adam called every living creature, that was the name thereof.

²⁰ And Adam gave names to all cattle, and to the fowl of the air, and to every beast of the field; but for Adam there was not found an help meet for him.

²¹ And the LORD God caused a deep sleep to fall upon Adam, and he slept: and he took one of his ribs, and closed up the flesh instead thereof;

²² And the rib, which the LORD God had taken from man, made he a woman, and brought her unto the man.

²³ And Adam said, This is now bone of my bones, and flesh of my flesh: she shall be called Woman, because she was taken out of Man.

²⁴ Therefore shall a man leave his father and his mother, and shall cleave unto his wife: and they shall be one flesh.

²⁵ And they were both naked, the man and his wife, and were not ashamed.

Genesis 3 - King James Version

[1] Now the serpent was more subtil than any beast of the field which the LORD God had made. And he said unto the woman, Yea, hath God said, Ye shall not eat of every tree of the garden?

[2] And the woman said unto the serpent, We may eat of the fruit of the trees of the garden:

[3] But of the fruit of the tree which is in the midst of the garden, God hath said, Ye shall not eat of it, neither shall ye touch it, lest ye die.

[4] And the serpent said unto the woman, Ye shall not surely die:

[5] For God doth know that in the day ye eat thereof, then your eyes shall be opened, and ye shall be as gods, knowing good and evil.

[6] And when the woman saw that the tree was good for food, and that it was pleasant to the eyes, and a tree to be desired to make one wise, she took of the fruit thereof, and did eat, and gave also unto her husband with her; and he did eat.

[7] And the eyes of them both were opened, and they knew that they were naked; and they sewed fig leaves together, and made themselves aprons.

[8] And they heard the voice of the LORD God walking in the garden in the cool of the day: and Adam and his wife hid

themselves from the presence of the LORD God amongst the trees of the garden.

⁹ And the LORD God called unto Adam, and said unto him, Where art thou?

¹⁰ And he said, I heard thy voice in the garden, and I was afraid, because I was naked; and I hid myself.

¹¹ And he said, Who told thee that thou wast naked? Hast thou eaten of the tree, whereof I commanded thee that thou shouldest not eat?

¹² And the man said, The woman whom thou gavest to be with me, she gave me of the tree, and I did eat.

¹³ And the LORD God said unto the woman, What is this that thou hast done? And the woman said, The serpent beguiled me, and I did eat.

¹⁴ And the LORD God said unto the serpent, Because thou hast done this, thou art cursed above all cattle, and above every beast of the field; upon thy belly shalt thou go, and dust shalt thou eat all the days of thy life:

¹⁵ And I will put enmity between thee and the woman, and between thy seed and her seed; it shall bruise thy head, and thou shalt bruise his heel.

¹⁶ Unto the woman he said, I will greatly multiply thy sorrow and thy conception; in sorrow thou shalt bring forth children; and thy desire shall be to thy husband, and he shall rule over thee.

¹⁷ And unto Adam he said, Because thou hast hearkened unto the voice of thy wife, and hast eaten of the tree, of which I commanded thee, saying, Thou shalt not eat of it: cursed is the ground for thy sake; in sorrow shalt thou eat of it all the days of thy life;

¹⁸ Thorns also and thistles shall it bring forth to thee; and thou shalt eat the herb of the field;

¹⁹ In the sweat of thy face shalt thou eat bread, till thou return unto the ground; for out of it wast thou taken: for dust thou art, and unto dust shalt thou return.

²⁰ And Adam called his wife's name Eve; because she was the mother of all living.

²¹ Unto Adam also and to his wife did the LORD God make coats of skins, and clothed them.

²² And the LORD God said, Behold, the man is become as one of us, to know good and evil: and now, lest he put forth his hand, and take also of the tree of life, and eat, and live for ever:

²³ Therefore the LORD God sent him forth from the garden of Eden, to till the ground from whence he was taken.

²⁴ So he drove out the man; and he placed at the east of the garden of Eden Cherubims, and a flaming sword which turned every way, to keep the way of the tree of life.

⸎

Footnotes

[1] Unless otherwise stated, all biblical quotations are taken from the King James Version (KJV) of the Bible

[2] https://www.etymonline.com/word/Eden

[3] ibid

[4] Genesis 3:22

[5] Genesis 3:6

[6] Strong's Concordance 7919

[7] Genesis 3:6

[8] And the Lord God commanded the human, saying, "From every fruit of the garden you may surely eat. But from the tree of knowledge, good and evil, you shall not eat, for on the day you eat from it, you are doomed to die." Page 8, Alter, R. (1998). *Genesis*. W.W. Norton.

[9] Ecclesiastes 12:1-6 is but one of many examples and it contains many idioms worth exploring.

[10] Lamsa, G. and Lamsa, G., 1985. *Idioms In The Bible Explained*. San Francisco: Harper & Row.

[11] In Hebrew the words *tov v'rah* 'good and evil' are an idiom for 'all things'. From Rabbi J. H. Hertz commentary on Gen 3:5 *Pentateuch and Haftorahs*, Soncino Press London 1937

[12] Genesis 2:16

[13] Genesis 3:17

[14] Genesis 3:16

[15] Genesis 2:16

[16] Genesis 2:17

[17] Genesis 3:17

[18] Genesis 3:5

[19] Genesis 3:1

[20] Genesis 2:7

[21] Page 62, The Book of J, Rosenberg, David. and Bloom, Harold. 1990. New York: Grove Weidenfeld.

[22] Genesis 2:17

[23] The New Testament according to the Eastern Text, George M Lamsa, 1940, p.xxiv and note on Matthew 19:24.

[24] George M. Lamsa, The Holy Bible from Ancient Eastern Manuscripts (Philadelphia: A. J. Holman, 1957) vii–viii

[25] The term, "eye of a needle," is a Hebrew idiom for "*any task requiring great skill and focus.*"

[26] Genesis 3:11, 3:17

[27] Genesis 3:16

[28] Genesis 3:17-19

[29] Genesis 3:12

[30] Now when He was asked by the Pharisees when the kingdom of God would come, He answered them and said, "The kingdom of God does not come with observation; nor will they say, 'See here!' or 'See there!' For indeed, the kingdom of God is within you."; Luke 17:20-21

[31] His disciples said to him, "When is the kingdom going to come?" <Jesus said>, "It is not by being waited for that it is going to come. They are not going to say, 'Here it is' or 'There it is.' Rather, the kingdom of the father is spread out over the earth, and people do not see it."; 113 Thomas Gospel (Layton)

[32] Luke 23:39-43

[33] Luke 23:41

[34] Mark 15:27-32

[35] Mark 15: 27, 15:32

[36] Luke 23:42

[37] 2 Corinthians 12:4

[38] Revelation 22:1-2

[39] Ezekiel 36:9

[40] Matthew 6:14

[41] Matthew 22:35-40, Mark 12:28-34, Luke 10:25-28, Deuteronomy 6:4-5, Leviticus 19:18